I GIVE YOU MY HEART

A TRUE STORY OF COURAGE AND SURVIVAL

WENDY HOLDEN

ISBN: 9789493231726 (ebook)

ISBN: 9789493231719 (paperback)

ISBN: 9789493231733 (hardcover)

Publisher: Amsterdam Publishers, The Netherlands

info@amsterdampublishers.com

I Give You My Heart is part of the series: Holocaust Survivor True Stories WWII

CONTENTS

AUTHOR'S NOTE

This book is based on a true story, as remembered by the few who lived through the experience and were able to keep it secret. Their tale has survived the decades thanks to the determination and resilience of a handful of people who preserved some poignant physical evidence. The author is indebted to these custodians of memory. Where precise conversations or exact details cannot be recalled, they have been recreated from the information available – with the blessing of the survivors and their families. Some names have been substituted for those forgotten or unknown. The sequence of events, as chronicled in this account, remains unalloyed.

This book is dedicated to two incredible women –
Zula and Ella

FOREWORD

I don't remember how old I was when I first heard about the Holocaust. As a child, I knew that my parents had lived through a horrible tragedy and suffered great loss. I was also vaguely aware of a remarkable story in my mother's past, about a brave mother figure in Warsaw, Poland, and the teenage girl whose life she had saved.

That teenager was my mom, Ella Frenkiel Złotnik, and the woman who sheltered her was Zofia 'Zula' Pieńkiewicz. Over the years, more information came to light as my mom shared fragments of her memories with me. I also absorbed more information from overheard conversations between her and her girlfriends who'd also survived the war. I learned so much from my mother. She taught me about love, tolerance, empathy, forgiveness and humanity.

As a little girl, the character of Zula loomed large in my mind as a shining beacon of light, representing all that was good. I was seven years old when I finally met her. Zula walked into our New York apartment on my mother's arm, straight from the airport, but wasn't at all as I'd imagined. The person in front of me didn't have the mythical proportions I expected; she was an ordinary older woman (54 years), much shorter than I'd expected, with a warm face, smiling eyes who did not speak a word of English. From then on, I remained glued to her side, smitten. Even though I'd never met her before, it felt completely natural to call her 'Grandma' as she was the closest to a real grandmother that I had.

Although these two women lived more than 4,000 miles apart, Zula was never far from my mother's thoughts and their loving, long-distance relationship lasted until their dying days. Despite the difficulties of communicating with or travelling to a country behind the Iron Curtain during the Cold War, my mother visited Zula several times over the years and was at her bedside during her final days. By the time my mother's health began to fail many years later, it was too late for me to ask her more about her wartime experiences or delve deeper into her memories of the past.

Now I am a mother to Danielle, Ilana and Ari, a mother-in-law to Ron and Shai, an aunt to Josh, Rissa, David, Alexa, Griffin, Malin and Jake, and a grandmother to Leor, Ella, Yuval, Liv, and Maya. I feel compelled to unearth as much as I can about the lives of Zula and Ella, and to pass on their remarkable legacy from generation to generation.

I am indebted to Zula's daughter Jowita Pieńkiewicz for providing me with as many detailed accounts as she could – some 60-odd pages of testimony that has proved invaluable to the chronicling of my mother's story. Jowita also kindly accompanied author Wendy Holden and me on our numerous trips into the past, both geographically and figuratively, several of which were not easy for her to take. Jowita once told me, "You deserve this history. I will try to describe for you a history of an acquaintance between two families and the conditions of their everyday lives."

I am exceedingly proud and happy that the details of Jowita's remarkable testimony, supported and enhanced by Wendy's research as well as the interviews that my mother participated in, are now presented so beautifully in this book. It is a love letter to Zula and Ella, two women who refused to let their differences separate them or the darkness of their times destroy them.

I Give You My Heart honours them both.

I could never have embarked on this journey if not for the love and support of my husband Mark and our three children. Their constant encouragement, pushing me to follow my dream of seeing this story written has made it possible for me to lead this project to completion. I would also like to acknowledge several people who helped me in various capacities along the way during the past few years. I thank my brother, Mitchel Perkiel, for contributing his memories and impressions. My sincere gratitude goes to Nadia Ficara at the United States Holocaust Memorial Museum for taking such an interest in this story and for introducing me to Wendy. Thanks also go to Igor Pietraszewski, Dvora Negbi Meneshof, Aline Grossman, Olimpia Novick Sulla, and Andrzej Puchacz for all they did to assist me during the writing of this book.

And, of course, I am especially grateful to Wendy Holden. When we first met, I knew that I was meeting an extraordinary human being. She has the innate ability to make everyone feel important and welcomed. Her research and writing talents were immediately obvious to me after reading her book, *Born Survivors*. I loved every moment of our collaboration.

Anita Perkiel Sarna, New York, USA

Warsaw, 1944

The Garden

The garden slept in the August heat
while in the distance the world silently fell.
I looked into the pale, tired faces —
I chose you as if I picked a flower.
Pale, passive, you came with me,
not even knowing why and where.
That bright morning for you was dark,
and everywhere strange and everywhere bad.
As days and months passed,
you grew into my heart through fear and tears...
Surely now in no separation
will I forget you or you me.
I once promised that I will save you,
That I will guard you as my own,
God will forgive me that I don't defend you,
I, who is like a shard, like a thing.
Today is your holiday my little one —
The only present that I will give you:
Let my song sway you —
I give you my heart — it's all that I have.[1]

Zula

Pawiak Prison, Warsaw, July 1944

---

1. Written on a cigarette paper by Zofia Pieńkiewicz, a senior officer of the underground Polish Home Army, and smuggled out of a Gestapo prison shortly before she was sent to Ravensbrück concentration camp.

PROLOGUE

London, summer 1970

Ella recognised Jowita in the hotel lobby immediately. It wasn't just the coat she was wearing – Zula's old summer one that flared at the waist – it was her smile. Jowita had her mother's smile. Ella ran to embrace the visitor from Poland, hugging her warmly. For a moment her husband Romek, who stood watching, wasn't sure the pair would ever let go.

"I'd have known you anywhere, dear Jowita!" Ella cried, her eyes glistening.

"I thought wearing this might help you recognise me after so many years," Jowita replied.

"It suits you," Ella announced, immediately linking arms with the 38-year-old woman who was eight years her junior, before further admiring her outfit and the way she wore her hair.

Jowita returned the compliment and they both then commented on the green silk dress of a woman who hurried past them to the bar.

Romek, fascinated, coughed to remind them he was there. Ella introduced him apologetically before he tilted his head to ask, "And, remind me, when was it you two last saw each other?"

"April 17, 1944," the women replied in unison. Catching each other's eye, they both nodded in respectful acknowledgement of that fateful day.

"You were taken away in the middle of the night," Jowita added quietly, summoning up the long-buried memories of the teenager with the sad eyes she had come to think of as a sister.

"Yes." Ella squeezed Jowita's arm. "Yes, we were."

Romek laughed. "As long as I live, I will never understand women. 1944? That's nearly thirty years ago, yet the two of you behave as if you had lunch together yesterday. Come on now, ladies, talking of food – I'm hungry. Let's go and eat."

Still arm in arm, the two women followed him into the dining room of the Hotel Ambassador near Marble Arch in London, chatting continuously. Ella smoked her favourite Kent cigarettes through a silver cigarette holder beset with semi-precious stones that made her look even more like a film star. Jowita also thought that Romek, who had given up smoking, was so handsome that he looked like a Roman Caesar. She needn't have worried that she wouldn't recognise his wife – the pretty young girl who'd lived with them during the war. It wasn't just her eyes. "She hadn't changed much at all. She was a beautiful, very elegant woman with that instantly recognisable curly blonde hair."

Romek ate heartily that night, but his dinner companions barely touched their food. They had so much to catch up on – two old friends reconnecting in an atmosphere of mutual fondness. Jowita explained how she'd been allowed to visit the West thanks to a special permit. After hearing of her award-winning work in Polish television and radio drama, the British Council had invited her to visit some British theatres and TV studios to see actors at work. She was lodged in a student house in Oxford and had already visited the Royal Shakespeare Company in Stratford-upon-Avon.

Ella explained that she and Romek were also in the UK on business. They'd left their home in New York a few days earlier to travel to Europe for Romek's work and to visit some old friends. It was only when she contacted Zula's brother George in London that she discovered that Jowita would be in Britain for the first time the very same week. "I couldn't believe the coincidence! I was so happy to think we could meet again after all this time."

"Me too," Jowita replied with feeling. "It's been far too long."

Letting their food go cold in that busy hotel dining room, the women hardly took a breath in between chatting about everything from their children to their jobs, their homes and their friends, recounting which of their mutual acquaintances they'd kept in touch with since the war. Romek abandoned asking questions and listened attentively, trying to keep up.

"I have something to show you," Ella said, suddenly remembering. She reached into her purse and pulled out her wallet into which was folded a flimsy piece of paper, just like those used to make carbon copies of typewritten documents. "Have you ever seen this before?" she asked, her eyes suddenly clouded with memory.

Jowita took the fragile scrap with care as tiny fragments fell from its edges. Her hands trembling, she began to read her mother's distinctive handwriting, albeit in miniature. It was a poem entitled *The Garden* that Zula had written in the women's section of the notorious Gestapo prison of Pawiak in Warsaw during the war. Ella gently explained. "Your mother gave this to me in the cell we shared just before we were separated. Let me see, this must have been in July 1944... I have kept it with me ever since."

She watched Jowita's lips move silently as she followed the words Zula had written to Ella, the pretty teenage Jewish girl she had risked her life – and that of her entire family – to protect. Ella, the blonde-haired, blue-eyed child Zula had come to think of as her own. The poignant verse was written at a time of great uncertainty as the Red Army approached Warsaw and the Nazis were deciding which of their prisoners to execute first as they eliminated the witnesses to their atrocities. Its carefully chosen words indicated just how close the pair had become during their bitter incarceration.

Reading the poem together all those years later, it was Ella who crumpled first, and Jowita quickly followed. Shoulder to shoulder, they stared into the past. Jowita said afterwards, "We bent over that paper, hugged... and suddenly burst into tears... It was as if the restaurant disappeared. There were no elegant people staring at us with dismay – not even Romek. We had really met only in that moment, and war was with us once again.

She explained how Romek, who had survived several concentration camps, behaved stoically. "He waited out the first explosion, kindly reassuring concerned fellow diners who wanted to call for some help that all was well. He gave us water and tissues, paid the bill and took us upstairs to their suite. I do not remember anything else from that evening, besides that it was a real meeting, under Romek's care, and that the whole time we sat hugging each other like children in a bomb shelter."

There was one thing that Romek decided upon that night, as he sat listening to more details of the story he thought he knew. The remarkable tale of Zula and Ella needed to be told. He had tried to get it told once before, by inviting a journalist into their home, but the four-part report never gave the story its full justice.

Theirs was a drama of such courage and love, self-sacrifice and trust. It encompassed some of the worst events during the war and the horrors of the Holocaust. So much had been risked and so much lost, but for the sake of all those who'd survived and for the next generation – Romek and Ella's children as well as Jowita's son – it was vital that the story didn't die with the two women sitting before him, weeping bitter tears over a fragile scrap of paper that would one day crumble to dust...

1

MŁAWA, POLAND, 1938

Moshe Złotnik and Artur Pieńkiewicz made the unlikeliest of friends. Two of the most important men in their town, they met through business but grew to know each other better playing cards, long before their lives became inextricably – and fatally – linked.

Moshe was a successful grain merchant in the agricultural town of Mława in the district of Mazovia 130 kilometres north of Warsaw and not far from the border with Germany. He happened to be Jewish. Artur was the local banker who – with his wife Zofia, known to all as 'Zula' – were stalwarts of the Catholic community. They also hosted some of Mława's liveliest social events including regular games of bridge to which Moshe and his wife Tzipora, known as Celina, were controversially invited.

In the serious business of card playing in the salon of the Pieńkiewicz's elegant third-floor apartment, guests were supplied with generous quantities of food and wine, although the Złotniks politely refused everything because it wasn't kosher. Bridge had become immensely popular across Europe and was quite the fashion in Poland, where the free-spirited Zula invited anyone she liked. There would be one table of regulars on which Artur paired up with whoever needed a partner, and a second table of an assortment of ladies and gentlemen over which Zula would preside. The family living room would be full of smoke, laughter, and the sound of clinking glasses, all of which wafted along the corridor to the couple's two young children, Jowita and Kalina.

The bridge players varied from week to week but included the deputy district police commissioner, members of the Landowners' Club, local aristocrats, the Catholic priest and the Złotniks, many of whom Zula knew through her husband's banking connections. Her random selection of guests raised eyebrows even higher amongst Mława's elite. Under the strictures of pre-war sensibilities in Poland, any friendships or professional relationships between races and faiths were generally kept within the boundaries of the workplace and rarely extended to private homes. Religious ladies of the upper echelons, no doubt fuelled by gossip from their maids, considered it scandalous that what was considered a 'proper Catholic home' should dare to mix a priest with a Jew in a society where there were strict social and racial barriers.

Little did they know that many amongst the town's almost 8,000 Jews were equally offended. Just as Artur had to defend himself to those who questioned his associations with the Złotniks, Moshe came under similar pressure until he assured his fellow merchants that playing cards with the bank manager was merely 'good for business'. Władysław Maron, the friendly priest at Our Lady, Queen of Poland Church, had an even harder time convincing his bigoted flock that it was appropriate for him to attend a party where Jews were also invited. A man who earned the nickname 'Little Tomato' for his habit of turning bright red while concentrating on his hand, Father Maron – exasperated by the complaints he received about the Pieńkiewicz card games – eventually suggested that people host their own less scandalous parties if they felt so strongly.

What few people in the town knew was that Moshe Złotnik and his wife Celina were also invited, separately and alone, to intimate gatherings at Zula and Artur's home. As with the bridge parties they still couldn't accept any non-kosher food, but Moshe was permitted to drink a shot or two of vodka with his host, or even a glass of the famous *pesachovka*, a popular liqueur for Passover. They chatted about many things including arts, culture, music and books. Artur almost certainly told them about his purchase of a large plot of land in Mława on which he planned to build a house and garden for his retirement one day. And Moshe would have discussed the state of his business dealings in the area. These relaxed social invitations were reciprocated so that, on a handful of occasions, Artur and Zula put on their hats and coats and visited Moshe and Celina at their home just a short walk away.

The Złotniks were also the proud parents of two young children – Jochewed, known as 'Ella', and Yishayahu, known as 'Ishay' – the apples of their eyes. At 15 years old, Ella was already blossoming into a pretty young woman with blonde hair and pale blue eyes. From the earliest age, she was a girl in possession of enviable tranquillity. By contrast, her eight-year-old brother Ishay was red-haired, more heavily featured, and mercurial – much more like his mother. It was said by the servants that Celina Złotnik ran an exemplary household, something that would have undoubtedly impressed their guests. Ella certainly inherited her innate sense of style and decorum. Although Celina had been educated in a progressive Hebrew school and was not as Orthodox as her husband, their home was kosher espousing customs that would have been unfamiliar to their guests.

Despite the two communities living alongside each other for generations, most Catholics in Mława would only have had rudimentary knowledge of Jewish traditions. They'd have been aware of the main holidays and that Shabbat or Sabbath was kept every Saturday, beginning with the lighting of candles on Friday nights. They recognised the traditional black hats and coats of the most observant and knew that the brick-built meat market had two distinct sections for kosher and non-kosher products. They would have enjoyed Jewish delicacies in the local inns and restaurants, but those courtesies rarely extended to private homes, where the restrictions on what Jews could eat and drink discouraged normal socialising. Besides, no one ever did.

Mława had been alternately Polish, Prussian, German and Swedish during its long and troubled history. In the wake of the

First World War and the restoration of Poland to the Poles after 123 years of foreign rule, it was one of the towns earmarked for government investment to speed its revival. With a fast-growing population and industry based on distilleries, brickmaking, textiles and foundries, most of the town's 26,000 inhabitants still travelled in horse-drawn wagons. Their greatest excitements included two annual fairs, the direct train links to Warsaw and Gdansk and the daily market, which was busiest on Tuesdays and Fridays but closed every Saturday, on the Sabbath.

In one contemporary account of that period recorded in Jewish Gen, the resource for Jewish Genealogy, life in the town was vividly recorded and the market described as a hive of activity, with stalls of every description selling all kinds of food, livestock and other wares, as housewives and merchants jostled for the finest wares. There were musicians and fire-eaters, magicians, tailors and cobblers, with hundreds of horses and wagons tied up either side of the central church.

"On Tuesdays and Fridays all the streets breathed and seethed with the pulse of trade... From early dawn, peasants streamed into the market in carts harnessed to one or two horses. The carts were loaded with wheat, baskets full of fruit, geese, ducks, chickens, and turkeys. Here and there a pig or a calf was lying in the wagon, and tied to the back of the wagon, was a colt or a cow. The peasants who came on foot carried straw baskets filled with butter, cheese, cream in earthen pots, cherries, strawberries, or even fowl. One farmer led a cow, another, a flock of geese. In an endless din all these flowed into the marketplace from all directions... Usually quiet Jews changed so during market days that one did not recognise them. People forgot themselves entirely, and 'shed their skins'. Jewish men and women would run after a peasant and his cart... To lay hold of a sack of grain, or a cow, or a chicken was considered to one's credit.

"The main trade was in grain. A Jew would grab a wagon loaded with wheat and rush over with the peasant to a granary belonging to a big wheat dealer such as Moshe David Złotnik... and others. The middleman was paid his commission 'per sack' and then he would run out to look for another prospective customer with a wheat-laden wagon."

By contrast, on Saturdays and holidays the market rested, and all the stores closed. The few people seen about were Jews dressed in velvet and silk heading for the synagogue.

In this close community, anybody who came from outside Mława was a focus of attention and the young banker Artur Pieńkiewicz and his wife were no exception. It was Zula, however, who was the chief topic of conversation in the marketplace and behind closed doors. A beautiful and exotic young woman who'd had an unusual childhood; she was born in the city of Łódź on January 6, 1909, to a 33-year-old Russian noble Paweł Kalinin Karniewski and his 28-year-old Polish wife Jadwiga. Zula grew up in Warsaw, where her father was the manager of the Polish branch of the prestigious Russian bank Volga-Kama, and the family spent their summers on a beautiful estate in what was then part of Ukraine.

At the outbreak of the First World War in 1914, however, the Russian Tsar summoned the directors of all the state establishments, including Paweł, to the capital Petrograd (now St Petersburg) with their bank's treasures. He took his pregnant wife Jadwiga and five-year-old daughter Zula with him and settled in the town of Voronezh where he ran the Ukrainian branch of the bank. It was there that their son Jerzy or George was born. Once the Russian Revolution began in March 1917, dismantling the Tsarist aristocracy in favour of the communist Soviets, the Poles there were suddenly in grave danger. When armed militias took to the streets to hunt down and execute 'enemies of the people' – including the imperial family – Paweł and his fellow aristocrats fled back to Poland. In the chaos that ensued, and swept up in a tide of refugees, he became separated from Jadwiga and the children and was forced to go on without them. For the next five years his little family was trapped in Russia, enduring great poverty and epidemics, as well as the constant threat of being killed or sent to Siberia. Sharing one small property with other Polish families, Jadwiga – until recently a bank manager's wife – became their unofficial leader and bartered their most valuable possessions for food and firewood.

"She sold her pearl necklace for millet," her granddaughter

Jowita said. "They lived on those two sacks of millet and a barrel of sour cabbage or sauerkraut for an entire winter. They hid those who were struck down with cholera from the authorities (and certain death) and used ancient Siberian techniques to treat them." Throughout, Jadwiga somehow maintained her dignity and insisted on keeping up certain standards, providing lessons and books for the children. She even paid for an oil painting of Zula as a young girl by an impecunious artist with some of their precious food.

Zula spoke little about her years in Russia, apart from how inspirational her mother was. Jowita said, "I think it formed her in a way as a fighter; always ready to fight in defence of her own and other people's rights." There was one incident especially that inspired and emboldened her for the rest of her life. "A group of revolutionaries rode into their town, and everyone scattered. The only thing to do was not to be seen as a new battle broke out between the Trotskyists and a military unit. Mother was supposed to stay hidden, but she looked out to see a girl aged about ten astride a huge white horse, shooting indiscriminately. She was wearing silver spurs and beautiful suede boots and Mama was charmed for life. She wanted to be that girl, instead of hiding like a criminal. She never forgot her."

By the time the peace treaty was signed in 1922 and Jadwiga and the children could finally return to Warsaw, Paweł had changed his surname to Kaliniecki, which sounded more Polish. Thirteen-year-old Zula worshipped her father and was thrilled to be reunited with him. Her brother George, who spoke better Russian than Polish, refused to accept at first that this stranger was his father. He and Zula soon settled back into normal life, living in a beautiful apartment near their father's bank. They spent the summers in a cousin's country manor house and were privately educated in the city so that they could catch up on the schooling that they'd missed. Zula loved attending a proper school again and wore her smart grey uniform with pride.

The 20 years between the two world wars in Warsaw marked a golden era for the 'city of gardens and palaces', which became a powerful and envied capital and the so-called 'Paris of Central Europe'. The streets teemed with life and there were scores of cafés and theatres, as Varsovians of all religions, cultures and races thrived. After centuries of suffering, Warsaw was a city looking to the future, with the construction of entire districts to house its more than one million inhabitants. In such a time of optimism and hope, anything seemed possible. After leaving school with excellent results and a command of English and German, Zula enrolled at the University of Warsaw to read law. Much to the amusement of her family, she also joined the PPS (*Polska Partia Socjalistyczna*) or Polish Socialist Party with its avowed intent to 'fight for a better life for the underprivileged'. This decision to become what was dubbed a 'soft sofa socialist' at the time was no doubt sparked by her own life-changing experiences of poverty and hunger.

Those bitter years in Russia had also marked Zula's mother forever, and the family recalled one memorable night in Warsaw when that manifested itself most painfully. Jadwiga and Paweł had just left the opera house with friends when she spotted a pile of firewood that had accidentally fallen from a farmer's cart as it turned a corner. Oblivious to everyone else, she ran into the street in her finery and set about collecting logs, grabbing handfuls to carry home beneath her furs. Although the incident was considered embarrassing at the time, her compulsion to stockpile for fear of deprivation would ultimately save her and her family during the Second World War.

Paweł, a deep-thinking telepath who was interested in philosophy and religions, had meanwhile been asked to help set up a network of co-operative savings banks, one of which was in the town of Mława. The new organisation was known as the *Komunalna Kasa Oszczędności*, or KKO, which translates to Municipal Savings Bank. Paweł's chosen deputy was bright young Artur Pieńkiewicz from eastern Poland (now part of the Ukraine), whom he'd persuaded to leave his former employers before grooming him to take over once he retired. Artur's decision to work not just for the benefit of the aristocracy was in keeping with a wave of social reform following the First World War when, after more than a century of division between Prussia, Austria and Russia, Poland regained its independence and thousands returned home to help it flourish.

As was common in Central Europe during these troubled times, Artur also had an unusual childhood. The Russians had seized his family's estate in the 1800s and those relatives who weren't banished to Siberia were forced to live on what little land they had left. When the Revolution reached Ukraine in 1918, Artur was at a Jesuit boarding school in Simferopol, Crimea, where stories of the slaughter of the Polish gentry reached him. Aged 19 and accompanied by a group of boys from his neighbourhood, he went to find his family but servants from his household intercepted him and warned, "Master, do not go back. They are waiting for you with knives!" His parents, grandmother, three brothers and four sisters had all been beheaded. Their home was charred ruins.

Orphaned and homeless, Artur fled to his mother's family in Kiev and after two years he joined the Polish Army fighting the Bolsheviks. In 1919 he was injured, whereupon his friends helped him to Warsaw to continue his studies. Within a few short years he had risen to the role of president of Bank Ziemianski, known as the Landlords' Bank, where Paweł Kaliniecki spotted his talent. "My grandfather liked and respected this young man who had lost so much," said Jowita. "He was absolutely alone without a penny in his pocket and an interrupted education but still he had made something of himself. My mother, too, saw something special in him."

In the summer of 1927, 18-year-old law student Zula visited her parents at their temporary home in Mława for the first time. There she was introduced to 31-year-old Artur. As the boss's daughter, she was expected to socialise with her father's employees and especially with his protégée, who she'd heard was renowned as an excellent dancer and an accomplished sportsman. Zula's younger brother George was jealous of Artur's poise and prowess from the start, especially after he'd witnessed him on the dance floor. "He could, while dancing, bow down to drink a full glass of wine on the floor, and then dance some more," George reported, adding that he had never seen anything like it.

Artur considered the teenage Zula 'pretty and amusing', but initially thought nothing more of her than that. He was not looking for love and had no plans to tie himself down in marriage just yet. Although her studies and her friends were all in Warsaw, Zula suddenly showed great interest in visiting Mława and travelled there almost every weekend and for the summer holidays. She quickly raised eyebrows as the only woman in town to smoke cigarettes and wear trousers (inspired by Coco Chanel), or sandals without stockings – all of which were considered suitable only for boys. Perhaps most controversially of all, she set her heart on marrying the handsome 'Mister Artur' before even discussing it with anyone, least of all him. She'd only known him for a few months when she announced this momentous decision to her parents.

"What?" her mother cried, horrified. "Well, what does he say?"

"I don't know," Zula replied with a shrug. "He doesn't yet know he's going to marry me."

Paweł said little but Jadwiga complained that Artur was an unsuitable match as he was without family, land, or money, and too old for their daughter. He was, she argued, too popular to be acceptable in the town's social circles.

News of her unexpected declaration opened Artur's eyes to this determined young woman he was growing increasingly fond of. Yet still he did nothing. Zula, not to be defeated, defiantly wooed him until he fell in love with her. She then declared to her parents that he would be the father of her children whether they allowed her to marry him or not. Hoping this was a passing infatuation, Jadwiga persuaded her husband to dispatch their lovesick daughter to study French culture and history at the University of Montpellier in the south of France. For the next 18 months Zula did as she was told, but she sent Artur a torrent of letters, marking what Jowita referred to as 'a beautiful page in their history'. When she heard that her cousin Wanda had been seen flirting with Artur in her absence, she immediately cut short her studies and returned to marry him. Artur was 34 on their wedding day in August 1929 and Zula was 21.

Once wed, the couple moved into a five-bedroom, first-floor apartment in a white stucco building at 7, Długa Street, two blocks from the main market square and a similar distance from Artur's bank. In a street full of old timber-framed houses, it was the only brick-built property and comprised six large apartments with every modern facility including electricity, bathrooms with running water and toilets. Zula's parents also provided them with a cook named Mrs Michalina (brought in from Warsaw), and a maid as Zula had known servants most of her teenage life and wasn't at all domesticated.

Like all the smart women in Mława, Zula still had her dresses made in Warsaw but as she had very small feet, she was delighted to find an excellent local shoemaker near the Old Market, a man named Ksawery Bieńkowski. She immediately ordered new shoes to match her trousseau. She even brought friends from Warsaw to be fitted for his excellent range of footwear, including exquisite leather boots for horseback riding and hunting. The family had a radio but no telephone and no car, as there were few of either available in such a rural market town. Only the mayor and the police commissioner had both. Instead, people used horses for transportation and the clatter of hooves on cobblestones was the daily reveille.

Zula nevertheless did her best to embrace the life of a provincial banker's wife. She worked with Artur to help revitalise the town and did her best to befriend the female stalwarts of the Circle of Polish Ladies and the local branch of the Red Cross. She left both organisations in the end, dismayed by their narrow-mindedness and dismissing their members as 'dazed'. With Artur's blessing (and his financial backing) she set up a weekly journal, writing articles that campaigned for local causes, but the magazine failed to find readers. Missing the buzz of the city and her social life, she enrolled instead at the Department of Philosophy at Warsaw University and travelled there regularly to attend lectures and see plays and exhibitions with friends.

Artur worked long hours and was often on call night and day for his demanding new clients. With his indomitable young wife by his side, he became even more popular in the town for his gentle manner and persuasive ways. Most people in the area had traditionally kept their money in the linen closet, under the mattress, or behind a holy painting, so it took someone they really trusted to persuade them to deposit it instead into a savings account. Business was so good that the bank moved into bigger new premises twice more, first on Maja Street and then to the corner of Chrobrego Street.

At weekends and in the summer, the couple found time to enjoy riding, sailing, swimming and tennis. Artur was also the unofficial dance leader for the area's carnival balls – leading the marching *Polonaise* and the classic folk dance, the *Mazur*. Both Artur and Zula were accomplished shots, and each won awards in local shooting competitions organised by the Union of Reserved Officers. When their first child was born at home in Mława, she was a girl who was to be named Eva, but she lived for only a few minutes. To begin with she didn't breathe or make a sound so when she finally cried out, the doctor threw her up into the air with joy, but then failed to catch her. Baby Eva fell to the floor and landed on her head, killing her instantly.

Seeing how distraught their family doctor was at his own foolishness, Zula immediately declared that it was an unfortunate accident. "Please don't despair," she told him. "I will have another baby within the year." In spite of her gracious forgiveness, the doctor never recovered from the shame. He was unable to return to work and couldn't even bear to see Zula in the street for trembling, crying and apologising. He eventually retired, went mad, and ended his days in a psychiatric clinic.

Within two years Zula gave birth to her daughter Jowita on December 19, 1932. She was born in Warsaw's finest hospital, something Artur insisted upon after Eva's death. Zula recovered quickly from the birth and was blessed with so much milk that she volunteered to be a wet nurse to a baby in an adjacent room whose milkless mother had waited ten years for a child. The doctor who asked for her help suggested that she collect her milk in a bottle so that they could give it to the boy. Zula replied, "Why collect it? Bring him here. I'd be grateful to him as much as he would be to me." The doctor hesitated. "I must warn you that the baby boy is Jewish," he said, whereupon Zula laughed and replied, "You think he will bite me?" The child, Yitzhak, thrived on Zula's milk for many weeks and the family were eternally grateful. Zula even agreed to the child's grandfather watching him feed and said afterwards, "He was such an imposing man – a truly mighty person – that I felt like standing up and bowing. When he saw his grandson's face sucking at my breast, he almost wept." Sadly, she later lost touch with the family when the baby was weaned, and always wondered what happened to Jowita's little 'milk brother' that she'd gladly suckled.

Once she was a young mother, and with baby Kalina – known as 'Dola' or 'Dolenko' – born not long afterwards, Zula had to give up her philosophy studies and focus instead on running the household (with help), while trying to raise the next generation of independent women. Jowita was a sickly, thin and anaemic child, however, who spent a lot of time in hospital. She recalls a fun, loving but mercurial mother who veered from being very maternal to being rather aloof. "We never knew from one day to the next which she would be, and I think that made me rather nervous." On Zula's best days, Jowita remembers listening to her fantastical stories while being washed in a large basin. The children greatly anticipated the Saturday bath for which water was heated on the coal-fired furnace. As her health improved and she became more spirited, Jowita needed a wash more than most, as her best playmate was a huge Swiss mountain dog that lived downstairs, whom she called *Kochanie* (sweetheart). And famously once, when her grandfather visited from Warsaw in his car – a rare sight in Mława – she joined some other children sliding down its (filthy) curved wheel arches – wearing her best white dress for church.

Zula found the role of banker's wife mildly amusing. Her new status didn't stop her turning heads, and her avant-garde style – based on Paris fashions – continued to cause consternation amongst the female bastions of Mława. These women frowned upon the director's wife parading around town in what they considered to be men's clothing, smoking a cigarette through a long filter, and wearing a beret rather than a 'decent' hat. To add insult to injury, Zula openly used a skipping rope in the park with her children, entered men-only sports competitions, and paid her servants more than the going rate. Controversially, she supported her unmarried maid financially and emotionally when she fell pregnant and invited other members of her staff to music recitals and dances. This was shocking.

Missing her busy social life in Warsaw, Zula tried to rebel against the fixed schedules of her husband's life. Artur went to work at the same time every day and came home at precisely the same hour to be served lunch the moment he returned. His soup had to be waiting hot on the table so that it had cooled enough to eat by the time he'd washed his hands. Zula would complain that she missed him and would try to persuade him to alter his routines, but Artur handled her perfectly, silently rising from the table and going to his club if she was petulant or behaved badly. Jadwiga always said that only Artur and Paweł could control her wayward daughter and Jowita agreed. "When Daddy lost his temper, everyone went quiet. He would put on his hat and go for a walk. He didn't need to shout. Mama was much more capricious. She lived in a bit of a fantasy world and was easily bored."

As a child, Jowita remembers how her father liked to take a ten-minute power nap after lunch, from which he would wake fully refreshed. One day she found him asleep in his study, so she tied little red ribbons in his hair as he dozed on obliviously. He was woken only when the wife of a customer called unexpectedly to speak to him privately. He greeted her in his study, not realising why she seemed unsettled throughout their meeting until he glanced in the mirror.

It was Zula's determination to have more fun that led her to organise social events at their home in the evenings and at weekends. And it was her growing fondness for Celina Złotnik that led to the two couples meeting more often. 'Mrs Zula' especially liked the quiet, dignified ways of 'Mrs Celina', this well-read woman who was becoming her friend. They contrasted with her husband Moshe, a lively man with the sharp sense of humour who insisted on addressing Artur as 'Mr Director'. Both women had learned how to enrich their lives with reading at a time when books weren't that easy to come by. They read the literary press and shared whatever volumes they had, searched for, and imported new editions from Warsaw or Europe, and enthusiastically discussed those they enjoyed the most. Celina spoke and read French, a language and literature she was passionate about, and was delighted to meet someone who had lived in France and was fluent.

Although the Złotnik family mostly spoke Yiddish at home, Celina and Moshe also spoke excellent Polish and the two couples conversed easily. Ella Złotnik had picked up her parents' educated way of speaking just as effortlessly, although her brother Ishay still spoke Polish with the heavy Yiddish accent that was common amongst his fellow pupils at the Jewish school he attended. Neither child would have socialised much with the visiting adults, however, as children their age were considered virtually invisible until they were 15 and old enough to hold an intelligent conversation. A popular saying of the period across all faiths was that 'children and fish do not have a voice'.

Similarly, Jowita and Kalina Pieńkiewicz were kept under the strict supervision of their female governess, a spinster in her forties named Maria Grzębska known to them all as *Panna* Maria (Miss Maria) or – more familiarly 'Pamaja' because that was how Kalina said her name. She was the daughter of a seamstress from a local family of artisans, and the sister-in-law of Zula's favourite shoemaker Mr Bieńkowski. Artur had put the Bieńkowski's son Stanislav through college when he realised that the bright young boy would benefit from a better education than Mława could offer him. He funded everything from his books to his accommodation, and his faith in the boy was proved right – Stanislav went on to become an excellent teacher and, ultimately, the director of Mława's high school. The shoemaker and his wife were eternally grateful for Artur's generosity.

Pamaja not only taught the children, but she also ran the household for Zula, a role that gave her a higher status. As such, she took her meals with the adults, instead of with the servants or the children. She was soon considered a member of the family, giving orders to the domestic staff, and helping with the frequent parties that she enjoyed almost as much as Zula did. Pamaja also ensured that the children were clean and presentable if ever they were introduced to visitors such as Mr and Mrs Złotnik in the parlour or their father's study, where they would file in silently with clean hands and combed hair to bow and curtsey. As was the custom, the children would have referred to their parents' guests as *Pan* for Mr and *Pani* for Mrs but would only have met them once or twice, as they had little contact with their father's work unless he took them with him to his bank or to visit the businesses of his clients, where they'd be plied with sweets.

Jowita said later, "I couldn't describe the faces of Mr and Mrs Złotnik. It is more of an impression. She was very nice, quiet and smiling. We had to make an appearance and politely answer some questions and then we would be dismissed. I never saw them again, and think they only came when we were at school. They were never there for my father's Name Day, for example."

Jowita also recalls being allowed to see her father at his place of work, and how impressed she was. "He had a huge office with an enormous desk. To get to it we had to walk through a large anteroom full of tables with lots of ladies tap-tap-tapping away on their typewriters. Whenever we walked in, they all stopped typing to look up and smile, and then they started again. I have an old typewriter I found in the garbage years later just to remind me of that happy time."

The divisions between the communities and between classes ran deep and each family had its own world with its own customs, languages and clothes. Jowita and Kalina were never allowed to play in the courtyard behind their apartment block, for example, because that was where the poorer children played. In pre-war Europe, a person's headgear alone could identify their wealth and status, with peasant women in scarves and their menfolk in cloth or leather caps, while gentlemen and ladies always wore hats of quality and distinction, while Jews wore yarmulkes. Even though the children from each household lived not far from each other, and – later – attended schools on the same street, they would only have met occasionally in town or in the elegant, tree-lined Miejski Park at the weekends. This was a place for walking and meeting, known to the locals as the 'Mława Salon' where children of all classes (under the strict supervision of governesses) would push a wooden wheel along with a stick, or play with a ball.

The children might also have met in the town's sweet shop, run by a Jewish man with a huge beard, who sold the best confectionery. Jowita's favourites were called *krówka,* which means little cow. They were soft and made of milk, cream and sugar.

The Złotnik family had official residency status in the town, a privilege that had only been granted to Jews in Mława in relatively recent times in their 400-year history of living in the area. Previously, Jews had been forced to reside in the suburbs or nearby towns, build their synagogue on the fringes, and lay their dead in a dedicated cemetery some distance from where any nobles might be buried. It was only when Jewish merchants, craftsmen and textile workers started to bring real wealth to the region that a select few were finally allowed to live and work in its heart.

All the shops in Mława's market square belonged to Jews, apart from a bakery and two pharmacies. Moshe Złotnik was one of the town's most prestigious merchants whose impressive square-fronted shop named *Ziemipłody*, which means crops, stood in Stary Rynek, the main market square, opposite the Catholic church. There was a large wooden grain store at the rear of Moshe's premises with a hoist to lift sacks from the horse-drawn wagons that brought fresh produce into town from the surrounding countryside. Granaries built of wood or stone could be found in all parts of the town, according to the town's memorial site: "*Wherever you turned there was a granary covered with an awning and on all sides, doors like open mouths waiting to receive the abundant wheat from the fertile fields of Mazowsze. Jewish commission agents, buyers and sellers of second-hand goods, merchants, porters, wagonners and craftsmen were to be found there. A great portion of the city's inhabitants made a living from dealing in wheat."*

From the front of his prominent shop, Moshe could be found enthusiastically selling his grain. His fellow Jews who escaped to British Mandate Palestine remembered him as a man who stood out from the crowd. As an established merchant, he exported much of his grain to Germany through the Polish seaport of Gdansk more than 200 kilometres away. Mława was a hub between Prussian and Russian territories, and this journey was made very much easier by the direct train links that had been established relatively recently, even though the goods had to be transferred between wagons because of the differing railway gauges. Every afternoon the train from Warsaw would arrive, carrying the day's newspapers, which were eagerly awaited in town. The newsagent would carry them the three miles from the station on his wagon and be set upon by all those hoping for a copy. There were never enough to go around, so clusters of people would gather round those who read the news aloud for the growing crowd, adding their own comments, as men jostled and jeered each other good-naturedly.

Ella Złotnik remembered her childhood in Mława as 'a very cosy life', adding, "I have a very nice and warm feeling when I talk about my parents and growing up. It was very secure and very good." Well protected, she was blissfully unaware of any antisemitism in the town, even though the local newspapers did report some clashes between Catholics and Jews on market days, and a handful of people – no doubt riding the wave of national socialism that was taking over Germany – attempted to switch the main market day to a Saturday knowing that no Jew could attend. Instead of openly defacing the windows of Jewish shops with yellow stars or the word *Zÿd* or *Jude* for Jew, as had happened elsewhere across Europe, several of Mława's Gentile shop owners put up signs in their own windows, openly declaring their Catholic faith.

Ella attended a Jewish primary school and then a Jewish high school on Sienkiewicza Street, close to the park, where she was well educated, learning Hebrew but still mostly speaking Polish without a Yiddish accent, which was to prove vital later. The family was well supported and surrounded by grandparents, aunts, uncles, and cousins, all of whom contributed to their general sense of safety and confidence. Ella's paternal grandparents Isak Złotnik, a merchant, his wife Miriam and son Efraim lived in Raciaz, the town where Moshe was born less than 50 kilometres away. Her maternal grandfather, Avraham Mendel Frenkiel, ran a wholesale grocery store in Płocka Street, Mława, next to a bookstore owned by other relatives called Blum. They all lived close to the town's synagogue on Kozia Street and just blocks away from Moshe's shop.

Grandfather Frenkiel spoke Yiddish and only switched to Polish when he had to. He was so observant that he wouldn't even drink a glass of water in Moshe's home on the grounds that their housemaid was a Gentile, which in his view rendered everything she touched non-kosher. In many other ways, though, he was less conservative – allowing three of his children to emigrate to British Mandate Palestine in the 1920s and 30s and reportedly being a pushover when it came to his daughters' costly shopping trips to Warsaw. According to one relative, "The father would object, the mother would take to bed pretending to be ill, and then the father would accede."

Ella's mother Celina was involved in several local organisations including the progressive Jewish school she sent her daughter to, and the Parents' Association in which Moshe was an executive member. A staunch Zionist and a member of the secular Jewish youth movement Hashomer Hatzair as a young woman, she'd been instrumental in the emigration of her two younger sisters Dvora and Lonia to Palestine and had initially planned to join them. Ella said, "She was the one who pushed out two sisters and a brother to Israel. They left as *halutzim* (pioneers to establish a settlement) before the war... She was planning that when I finished tenth grade after four years in the *gymnasium* (school) that I would go to study in Palestine." Celina's brother Natan left on the eve of the war while another, Gershon, went to Liège, Belgium to study for his doctorate. The subject of his dissertation was 'Benevolence Amongst the

Jewish People'. On his return, he taught French to children in Mława. A third brother was Yaakov, about whom little is known.

Marriage and then motherhood permanently curtailed Celina's hopes for Ella to go to Palestine, which must have pleased her father at the time. Although he understood the fear and mistrust that the increasingly antisemitic politics of Europe had triggered in the younger generation, he disapproved of their zeal for a more secular life elsewhere. Her father was terribly against it. Like many of his generation, he saw their exodus not as a religious and spiritual return to the homeland, but as a desire to escape from centuries of prejudice unencumbered by tradition. He was right and when he and his wife eventually applied to emigrate to Palestine too, shortly before the war began, his two daughters – who were by that time working alongside men building roads, planting citrus trees and growing tobacco – prevented them from coming. According to the granddaughter of Celina's sister Dvora, "They did not want their parents to know how far they had strayed from religion."

Little did they know the consequences of their actions. Their youthful enthusiasm for a new world away from traditional Jewish life in Europe would ultimately save them from the horrors to come, but their decision to dissuade their parents at the eleventh hour would ultimately cost the older couple their lives.

2

INVASION. SEPTEMBER 1, 1939

"Before the world even knew we were at war, we had casualties, the Germans were already attacking us directly with cannons and people were being killed," Ella Złotnik told friends and family. The black events of Friday, September 1, 1939, would remain engraved on her heart for the rest of her life. They marked the end of her childhood.

The horror that unfolded that morning came about initially as an accident of Mława's geography. Poland was almost completely landlocked between its biggest neighbours Germany and Russia but also bordered Czechoslovakia, Romania, East Prussia, Lithuania, and Latvia, placing it in an unenviable position on the European map. The town of Mława had the misfortune of being just seven kilometres from the East Prussian border. Fear of an impending Nazi invasion had been consuming the Poles since Hitler unexpectedly annexed Austria in the *Anschluss* of March 1938. After *Kristallnacht* (the Night of the Broken Glass) that November in which Jewish homes, businesses and synagogues were ransacked and destroyed across Germany with hundreds killed and injured, war was all anybody talked about. As diplomacy failed and the Nazis seemed unstoppable, escape plans started to be hatched.

The government made plans too. Several weeks before the outbreak of the Second World War, Polish army units took positions in Mława in case of attack, although the belief then was still that hostilities would be brief and involve only an attempted land grab. Marshal Edward Rydz-Śmigley, Commander-in-Chief of Poland's armed forces, assured everyone that not only would Poland not surrender the Danzig corridor, but they would not give even an inch to Hitler. In July 1939, Polish state radio issued instructions on how to detect mustard gas (it smells like garlic), use gas masks, protect windows and hang blackout curtains. Those without radios heard the orders via trucks that toured the streets blaring them out from special speakers. Fearing an impending attack, citizens descended on local stores for basic foodstuffs, leaving shelves stripped. As tensions rose, Jews and Catholics alike left town, fleeing to Warsaw or anywhere that felt safer.

Moshe Złotnik also left Mława the previous weekend. Carrying his wife's best jewellery and plenty of cash, he hurried to Warsaw to find a place for his family to live should the Germans march into Poland. He promised anxious Celina that he'd return soon, after making sure she had enough money and provisions should she need to scoop up their two children and join him. In the bustling capital, Moshe found an apartment in a good district at 3 Ogradowa Street and equipped it with all that the family might need, including cans of soup and sardines, sacks of flour and other basic provisions. Finding a telephone, he managed to pass a message to his wife on the night of August 31, 1939, to tell her of his success, adding confidently, "Don't worry. In Warsaw they say that war isn't coming soon. Maybe never. So, you can relax."

Within hours, he was proved fatally wrong. As the government feared, Mława was a key entry point for the invading Wehrmacht. In the early hours of the first day of September, the Germans brutally ended the golden era for Poland. They bombed the town, spreading fire and panic. The first victim was a young Jewish boy named Chanoch Zilberberg. When the region's water supplies were hit there was nothing with which to extinguish the fires, so buildings burned unchecked. During a short lull in the bombardment, most of the population fled to nearby towns such as Szrensk, Przasnysz and Strzegowo – many losing their lives along the way. Within three days, the Germans had captured Mława, which meant that anyone left alive was now a prisoner of the Nazi regime.

Celina Złotnik was forced to put their escape plan into action very early that morning. Grabbing her children and whatever she could carry, they set out towards Warsaw. Thanks to Moshe's preparedness, they must have been one of the few families to get out of the region safely by rail. The journey of 126 kilometres took two days, as their train stopped and started en route while waves of Luftwaffe planes attacked the tracks and stations with the avowed intent of crippling the country. Despite facing numerous dangers, Celina somehow succeeded in getting her children to the apartment where Moshe was anxiously waiting.

Back in Mława, life for their friends and family who remained would go from bad to worse. After the fighting ceased, many of the refugees returned home to discover an altered reality. The Germans had changed the name of their town to Milau to become part of *Bezirk Ziechenau* or the District of Ciechanów. In October, the Nazis drew up lists of all male Jews aged between 14 to 40, assigning each of them an ID number that they were ordered to wear prominently on their chests. Every day, several hundred of these men were selected for forced labour, while others were randomly snatched from the streets and sent away for the same purpose. After a while, the ID tags were changed to white patches and then to yellow stars emblazoned with the word *Jude* which had to be sewn onto their outer garments over their hearts and on their backs – like a target. By the end of 1939, all Jews in Poland were subjected to the same rules and countless other antisemitic Nuremberg Laws effectively banning them from public life. They were forbidden from walking on certain streets, travelling on public transport, or visiting parks and other public places. Bearded Jews especially were singled out for public humiliation and were beaten or forced to do demeaning tasks. During the holiday of *Sukkot* – the Feast of Tabernacles – the Germans rounded up all the town's Jews in the main square and threatened to deport them to the Soviet Union. The operation was only halted when a senior Nazi intervened.

Nevertheless, the persecution continued. One night in November 1939, German soldiers destroyed the town's synagogue, desecrating graves, along with two of Mława's *beth midrash* (Jewish houses of study) leaving them in flames. Those who tried to put out the fires were chased away. That same month, the Germans drove the Jews out from the three neighbouring towns of Dobrzyn, Drwecz, Sierpc and Rypin. More were to follow from Szrensk, Radazanów and Zielun. Most fled into Mława, where frightened locals took them in.

As in other Jewish ghettos which the Nazis were quickly setting up across Poland, they appointed a *Judenrat* (or Jewish Council) with Eliezer Perlmutter, the son of one of Mława's gristmill owners – and someone Moshe Złotnik would have known well – to be its Commissar. He was later murdered during an interrogation, but under his auspices, an official Jewish ghetto was established in the streets between Stary Rynek, the old market where Moshe had done business every day, Zdunska Street, and the deserted land bordering the Serecz River. To the east, the border ran along Warszawska Street and to the west along Płocka Street. The main ghetto gate was on Borzniecne, near the market, where a tall brick wall marked the boundary. Elsewhere, it was fenced off by wood or barbed wire, and any ghetto houses that overlooked 'the Aryan side' had their windows bricked in.

With a growing population of Jewish refugees, conditions in the ghetto deteriorated daily. An epidemic of typhus broke out, as people were crammed into every possible space including pigsties, basements, outbuildings, and attics. As the Nazi grip tightened, there were public executions, including four young men hanged for smuggling. The disabled or mentally ill were taken away and executed. When the first deportations of the elderly and sick to Treblinka and other Nazi death camps started to be carried out, many of the ghetto's occupants managed to flee just before it was completely sealed in 1941. Władysław Maron, the priest nicknamed 'Little Tomato' by Artur Pieńkiewicz, who remained in the town throughout the war, did all he could to save Jewish children from the gas chambers by issuing false baptism certificates for babies, stating that they were Catholic.

By December 1942, though, those trapped behind the barbed wire were beyond help, even from the priest. The ghetto was finally liquidated and the remaining 7,000 Jews were deported to Auschwitz, including relatives of the Złotniks who'd been unable to escape. At the end of the war, only 150 Jews from the town survived the camps and in August 1946, having reinterred the corpses of those murdered and erected a memorial to the dead, the last of Mława's Jews finally left the town.

For the Pieńkiewicz family, there was no sanctuary in being Catholic. Artur, Zula, and their children were also in grave danger immediately following the German invasion. Without knowing of the horrors that lay ahead, Zula confessed somewhat guiltily years later, "I know it's a sin to be glad that the war was beginning but I was glad at the first moment. In Mława I was choking with boredom."

In early August 1939, after a family holiday by the Bug River and its lakes near the Ukrainian border, the Pieńkiewicz's decided that Mława was too close to Prussia to be safe and sent Jowita and Kalina to stay with their grandparents Paweł and Jadwiga in Warsaw. Zula's brother George was also in the capital, completing his pilot's training at the school of airmen with a cousin, Zbyszek Osuchowski, whom he and Zula loved like a brother. Pamaja accompanied the children to the three-room apartment at 36, Genewska Street in the district of Saska Kępa. A summer break from their parents was an annual family tradition, but it was never more poignant that year as Artur and Zula waved them goodbye, fearing they all might come under attack at any moment.

Despite their fears (or perhaps because of them), the couple attended the housewarming party of the town's notary on August 31 – the night before the invasion. They drank, sang and danced with many of their friends including the local judge and the chief of police, with whom they often played bridge. The party went on until dawn and might have continued still longer but for the breathless arrival of a police officer sent to alert the group that at 04:15 the German army had broken the borders, attacked Poland without declaring war, and were heading south towards Mława.

Like many others at that party, Artur and Zula were already well prepared. "Father had always said there would be war and he was ready, but my mother didn't quite believe him," Jowita said. "Having lived through the First World War she couldn't bring herself to believe there'd be another." In near silence, the couple hurried home, packed their most precious belongings and documents into rucksacks, handed their apartment keys to the trusted janitor of Artur's bank, and mounted their bicycles for the long cycle to Warsaw. Zula was 30 years old and Artur 44. There were no trains running at that hour and they correctly suspected that all later transports would be stopped or attacked. Within hours, their town was occupied by the Wehrmacht and Gestapo officers who the following day began arresting the most important people according to lists drawn up for them by the handful of Germans who'd resided in the town for decades.

As elsewhere under Nazi occupation, those considered to be the most prominent were arrested, deported or killed to prevent them from stirring up any revolt. In addition, senior bank managers and those in charge of the public purse were arrested, tortured and forced to hand over all of a town's gold and other financial assets – an ironic situation given than the Polish złoty lost four-fifths of its value overnight. For both these reasons, Artur Pieńkiewicz was one of the first the Germans went looking for, but they found his apartment locked and empty. Instead, he and Zula were on a perilous journey that took them two days, hoping that at least in the capital their family would be together and relatively safe. Little did Artur know then that he would never see Mława again.

When Celina Złotnik finally reached Warsaw with her children by train during the opening days of the war she, too, must have been in a state of high emotion. Like her Catholic friends, she had left her home and her belongings behind along with many members of her family, her friends, and all that she'd ever known.

Their arrival in the city, whose citizens were in a panic, cannot have done anything to soothe her nerves. They didn't yet know that Hitler had specifically ordered his men to act without compassion in Poland, stating: "I have sent my Death's Head units to the east with the order to kill without mercy men, women and children of the Polish race or language. Only in such a way will we win the *Lebensraum* (living space) that we need." He had also signed a non-aggression pact with Russia that included secret clauses for the division of Poland.

The unprecedented aerial bombardment of Warsaw began in earnest on September 1 – a rain of bombs timed to coincide with German troops marching across the borders. Under the control of Hitler's deputy Hermann Göring, some 700 Luftwaffe aircraft bombed everything from the airport and military facilities to hospitals, schools, marketplaces and utility supplies, resulting in heavy human casualties. The so-called 'enemy' capital attracted special fury – mercilessly attacked by planes called *Stukas* that dive-bombed to earth, screaming their fury.

On September 8, Hitler's army marched on Warsaw in what seemed like a solid mass of steel. The first units reached outlying districts and the city was placed under siege. To begin with, the Polish defence forces valiantly held them back, destroying some 80 or so Luftwaffe planes but they were quickly pounded to dust and lost 70 per cent of their equipment and men. Within days, great swathes of the city were in ruins; its beautiful buildings and great landmarks vanished under teetering mounds of rubble and dust. No mercy was shown as civilians were strafed with machine gun fire and their bodies ridden over by tanks.

Nine days after Britain and France declared war on Germany, the Nazis demanded that Poland surrender but the Varsovians refused and continued to create barricades and create anti-tank defences. More than 20,000 volunteers took to the streets to dig trenches and defend Warsaw's traditions and beauty. Furious, Hermann Göring ordered still more aerial attacks, with round-the-clock bombing and incendiary devices that set the city alight. On September 17, the Soviets joined forces with Hitler and invaded Poland from the east, mustering 1.5 million soldiers and some 6,000 tanks. Defenceless against such a firestorm, Warsaw was doomed. "The city flows on the wings of flame and falls like a stone on the heart," wrote one Polish poet.

Besieged and beleaguered, sheltering in the basement of the flat that her father had found for them, Ella recalled later, "For two weeks we were surrounded by the Germans and couldn't buy anything, so we were lucky with our bags of mushrooms and barley."

Bombs rained down on them, and entire districts were ablaze. The corpses of humans and horses were abandoned where they fell as the smell of burning bodies choked the air and refugees roamed the streets looking for shelter. By September 22, all water, electricity and telephone connections were lost too, to be only partially reconnected later.

Capitulation eventually came on September 28, when – with an estimated 60,000 dead, much of the city destroyed, and food and water supplies all but depleted – Polish radio signalled defeat to its people by replacing the light-hearted *Polonaise* with a funeral march. The occupation, which was to last for a brutal six years and lead to the worst genocide in world history, had begun. Poland as a nation state had ceased to exist. Back in Germany, Hitler – who'd correctly gambled that the Allies wouldn't fight for Poland – ordered that every church bell in the Reich should be rung in celebration for a week. Swastikas replaced the white eagles and flags on every building left standing in Warsaw.

The Złotnik family might have prayed that even after occupation they could remain in their apartment, but their hopes were soon dashed. Hitler and Stalin partitioned Poland between the Germans and the Soviets and Krakow was declared the new capital. Warsaw became a separate entity under Hitler's personal lawyer Hans Frank, who was appointed Governor-General and Chief of Administration. As in Mława, a Jewish Council or *Judenrat* was forcibly established, and the city divided into Aryan and Jewish sectors for 'confinement' purposes. All Jews in Warsaw regardless of their status were compelled to move with only what they could carry and all Aryan Poles (and especially those of German extraction) were encouraged to move into the 'liberated' homes. At the same time, as many Jews as possible were rounded up from the countryside (including both sets of grandparents of the Złotniks) and were transported to Warsaw to join the city's hapless Jewish population.

Despite Moshe's valiant efforts finding his family somewhere to live, he could never have predicted that his haven lay beyond the new Jewish quarter's strictly defined streets. They had no choice but to pack up and start again, nervously wandering out into shell-damaged streets they no longer recognised patrolled by Wehrmacht soldiers and sinister columns of tanks. Ella explained, "Jews weren't allowed in other parts, so we had to leave as we weren't in the Jewish part. It wasn't a ghetto yet (that didn't officially happen until October 1940), it was just an area that Jews were supposed to live in, so we had to move first to an apartment at 60 Leszno Street and then to one at Karmelicka 7, in what became the ghetto. By the time we moved there, my father's parents came to live with us also from their small town. They had a little room with us. My other grandparents lived in Warsaw also, the whole family, but they didn't live with us at first. They had their own apartment."

The Nazis justified the compulsory movement of Jews into an area designated just for them as protection against growing antisemitism in the community. To begin with, many did feel safer there at a time of virulent anti-Jewish propaganda when Polish nationals were being pitched against them and the Germans started humiliating and victimising the most visibly observant Jews on the streets. Most, however, realised that this was the beginning of their imprisonment. Then the Germans claimed that the Jews would spread typhus and that they'd be contained in their *Wohnbezirk* or 'residential district' to protect the rest of the population. Their persecution was well underway and the vast tracts of land now under Frank's jurisdiction were secretly designated as the locations for Auschwitz, Lublin-Madjanek and Płaszów, as well as the death camps of Treblinka, Belzec and Sobibor. The Nazi mission was to 'finish off the Poles at all costs'.

The Führer hated Poland with a passion, seeing it as the home of Jews and Slavs and regarding it only as the place for his cherished *Lebensraum* into which he intended Germany to expand. Warsaw was especially reviled as the largest Yiddish-speaking community in Central Europe, boasting almost 400,000 Jews, constituting 30 per cent of the population. As the second largest Jewish community in the world after New York City it was also the political and cultural heart of European Jewry. Hitler visited Poland only once, on October 5, 1939, after which his deputy Joseph Goebbels wrote:

The Führer's verdict on the Poles is damning. More like animals than human beings, completely primitive, stupid, and amorphous. And a ruling class that is the unsatisfactory result of mingling between the lower order and an Aryan master race. The Poles' dirtiness is unimaginable. The capacity for intelligent judgement is absolutely nil.

At his behest, there were hundreds of mass executions and an estimated 6,000 people – including many Catholics – were shot in the early days of occupation. Those who were living in the Jewish quarter were also subjected to random shootings and beatings, and no one knew when it might be their turn next.

Daily life was getting harder and harder in the *Wohnbezirk*, especially for the children. Ella, then aged 15, resided in the same building as her mother's parents, the Frenkiels, who shared a room with others on the floor above them. She also made new friends at that same address, one of whom was Ala Biberkraut who lived with her mother Hanna, her brother Wladek, and father Benjamin, a jeweller.

Mainly to curb their constant hunger, the two girls took up smoking – whenever they could pinch a precious cigarette – and would slip out onto the balcony to smoke them in secret. This also gave them a chance to get away from their overcrowded rooms where there were always too many people who were equally tired and hungry, unwashed and grumpy, and constantly scratching from the fleas and the lice. Living directly above their balcony, Ella's grandfather smelled the cigarette smoke and quickly discovered what his granddaughter was up to. Realising that this was one of the few pleasures she had in such a miserable place, he asked only that Ella didn't smoke on the Sabbath.

Indulging in her secret vice again one night, Ella recalled an event she witnessed and would never forget. "When the ghetto was closed, we were not allowed to leave the house after seven at night because of a curfew, so we made friends in the building. One evening we were sitting on the balcony on the third floor facing the street at my friend's house. We were not supposed to be outside, but it was very dark and there were no lights, so it must've been about ten o'clock. Suddenly two German Jeeps came, one after the other, and stopped right in front of our building and grabbed someone – a man we didn't know – who was walking on the street. We saw everything. They put him up against the wall right across from us, and they just shot him there. We were even afraid to breathe. They left him for dead and drove away. We ran out and went downstairs and heard that someone pulled him inside the entrance, but he died."

With murders like these an everyday occurrence, Moshe and Celina were naturally very protective and did all they could to keep Ella and her little brother safe. Not that it was easy, as they had very little to offer them. Thanks to the Germans, they'd lost their house, their business, and everything they owned and only had what money and valuables they'd been able to take with them to Warsaw. Food and other goods were becoming scarcer and ever more expensive and the harsh realities of the family's new existence was beginning to bite. Records show that Celina's parents had to apply for charitable aid and free meals from the *Judenrat*, as – having fled from the Mława ghetto – they had even less.

Moshe Złotnik was a determined man as well as a born trader, however. Although he was more accustomed to selling his wheat in the market square, he was not a man to stand idle and watch his family starve. As Ella said later, "We lost everything we had in the town that we were in before, but my father was quite a capable man. Only now do I realise how capable he was. He started doing all kinds of business. He met someone in the jewellery industry, and they started buying and sending it out to the Christian side because people there were eager to buy it. Others were selling things too and he used to buy and sell them and make profits from the sales."

Moshe had spotted a need for someone like him as those in the Jewish quarter who had fled to Warsaw with their finest clothes, best jewellery, and leather-bound books quickly discovered that they needed to sell them to survive. Material possessions lost all value in a place where people were dying for want of bread. Heirloom rings, brooches, pearls, gold watches and necklaces that had often been passed down through families for generations were bartered for a fraction of their true worth in return for basic foodstuffs such as potatoes, bread, barley as well as warm clothing. Those who were selling precious items needed someone they could trust to help them broker a deal with those who had money beyond the quarter, and the Aryans who wanted to buy needed to have faith in the quality and provenance of their purchases. Moshe Złotnik was the perfect man for the job.

"He was supporting us quite nicely and also helping other people, especially close family, because his parents were living with us and the other grandparents and cousins, who were all starving. Every few days people came with their pots to get some of the food that my mother was cooking. She was always cooking for us, but also for other old people who came. My father worked hard to achieve this, and it was the only way he could make money. There were, of course, others who were starving, but we couldn't give food to everybody. But at least we could give it to those who were closest in the family."

It wasn't only food that was lacking in their lives. As Hitler had insisted that Poles were 'born just for heavy labour', all schools, colleges, and universities were closed to all races and faiths, unless they were German. Like so many other parents, the Złotniks were determined that their children shouldn't miss out on their education just because of the war. Ella, who was 15 and finishing the ninth grade, had hoped to become a pharmacist until the Nazis interrupted her plans. Everyone agreed that it was important that her studies continued as best they could, so she was sent to secret lessons organised privately in apartments by educators and volunteers who taught students in return for something to eat. The venues were changed daily to avoid being detected by soldiers or the police, and the classes were never too large as to arouse suspicion. "I was still going to high school. It was a continuation. I did everything as if in a normal high school, with tests."

Every day, conditions worsened in Warsaw. The two finest areas of the city centre were designated '*Nur für Deutsche* (Only for Germans)' – and its non-German residents forcibly evicted. Germans were the only citizens allowed to visit cinemas or theatres, galleries or libraries. All non-German businesses were requisitioned and placed in the hands of German overseers. The Nazis continued to organise random police roundups and street searches, sending people to labour camps, or executing them on the spot for the crime of not having the correct documentation, looking shifty or being 'an enemy of German reconstruction'. The disabled, sick and mentally unstable were sent away to be 'euthanised'. Any blond-haired, blue-eyed children considered 'racially worthy' were at risk of being snatched from orphanages or off the streets and sent to the 'Fatherland' to be adopted and raised as good German Aryans. This was part of the state sponsored *Lebensborn* programme designed to swell the Reich population with those who were 'racially pure and healthy'. Young women and unmarried mothers were, under the same SS-initiated scheme, encouraged to bear children for the Reich and, in some instances, forced into prostitution and raped by members of the SS to that end.

With these kinds of policies in place across occupied Europe, every time anyone in Poland or elsewhere stepped outside their front door they ran the risk of never returning home. If someone disappeared, their loved ones had no idea what had happened to them. They had to wait for the Nazis to post their lists of those condemned to death or slave labour, which were pinned to telegraph poles or lampposts. Only then did people know the worst.

Artur and Zula Pieńkiewicz arrived in Warsaw after their two-day cycle ride to find a city in crisis. They made their way to the apartment in the suburb of Saska Kępa, four kilometres east of the city centre, where Zula's parents Paweł and Jadwiga lived, and were reunited with their daughters. Her brother George and cousin Zbyszek had managed to flee the country and join Polish forces against the Nazis abroad, eventually travelling to France and then Britain where they enlisted as a navigator and a pilot for the RAF's 300 Squadron, based in Lincolnshire. Sadly, Zbyszek's Lancaster was shot down over Germany in 1944 and he was killed, along with most of his crew.

Along with every patriotic Pole, Artur was also determined to play his part. Armed only with his rucksack, he went looking for a mobilisation point in answer to the government's call for all capable Polish men to gather arms and form into military units. For the next six weeks Zula had no idea where her husband was, as she and her little family remained under siege from German bombardment. With no means of communication, she didn't know if he'd been killed, captured or was fighting on the front lines. Artur eventually returned after weeks of wandering all over Poland seeking military employment against the Nazis, only to discover a beaten and defeated army.

As penniless refugees, the family had no choice but to stay where they were and live on the dried bread that the resourceful Jadwiga had prepared for just such an event. Remembering her years trapped in Russia, since 1938 she'd been buying cabbages for *kapusta* or to pickle into sauerkraut, as well as meat to cure, and extra loaves that she sliced thickly, before drying and storing them in her pantry. This way, she managed to accumulate 12 sacks of her 'bread biscuits', along with a large pot of lard. Occasionally, they were able to buy or barter something else to supplement their diet as they waited out what they believed would be a short conflict that would end as soon as Poland's Western Allies came to the rescue.

That help sadly never arrived and the Germans came ever closer to Saska Kępa, reaching their side of the Vistula River early one morning about a week after the invasion.

Young Jowita will never forget that day, as her father took her to see the Germans marching through the streets. "He held my hand but as the soldiers marched past us, he squeezed it so tightly that I winced. He apologised for hurting me and pulled me away." A few days later, after Artur had once again gone looking for ways in which he could help resist the invaders, German soldiers appeared again, this time running through the streets shooting their guns and roaring *"Schneller! Schneller!"* The Wehrmacht was afraid of sudden attack from behind, so they ordered everyone out of their houses and told them to run to nearby villages across the fields. There were mostly old people, children and mothers left in Warsaw by then, but the Germans didn't care.

Realising that they were suddenly on the front line, Zula quickly helped her children and parents from their first-floor apartment, tripping over each other in the confusion. The family ran through clouds of red dust as houses fell around them and the streets were littered with the dead and dying. Once in the open, they found that the fields they were supposed to cross were so churned up by anti-tank trenches that they were virtually impassable. The Germans nevertheless shouted at them to keep going and when they reached the first trench and faltered, a soldier shot a hesitant young woman who fell headfirst into the ditch 'like a doll'.

In the middle of all this commotion, only Zula was calm. When she spotted an officer, she said something to him in a normal voice. She then quickly organised the group, giving them instructions to form a human chain with the tallest standing at the bottom of the trench to help the smaller, weaker ones cross. "Everyone did at once what she had ordered and soon, we were on the other side, the children passed from hand-to-hand across the trench, the adults helping one another through it. All of us except the young woman at the bottom of the trench who did not move any more."

By the time the group reached the neighbouring farms, where they found temporary sanctuary until it was safe enough to return, Zula was the one everyone looked to for answers. Again, she organised them all, seeking out accommodation, fresh milk and food. "She was serious and calm, solving one problem or another without hesitation. She was now the 'tower of strength', as she often used to call my father. Never before had I seen her ruling so deftly and with such cool sureness or getting people's attention so fast. This is how I remember her at her best."

Within a few days, the family returned to their home and Artur came back too. By then Warsaw was in ruins and what would prove to be a long, bitter winter was setting in. Hundreds of thousands of refugees had fled to the city after being forced from their homes and outlying farms by violence or decree. This ragged river of humanity discovered that German had become the official language overnight, the capital was now Warschau, and every street and institution had also been given a new German name. The Nazis ruled through terror and anyone could be shot on the spot for little or no reason. Most people were destitute, so the need for food and warmth dominated their daily lives. Thanks to the strict rationing that favoured German citizens, many survived only thanks to the soup kitchens set up by charitable organisations and the church. Furniture was burned for fuel and the black market provided food and coal for those who could afford the exorbitant prices. There were epidemics of TB and scarlet fever and the mortality rate soared.

Jowita, just six years old, recalled the winter of 1939/40 with great sadness. "That winter, hunger and fear hovered over Warsaw, and temperatures dropped to minus 40 degrees Celsius. The bridges were ruined, so people walked and even drove wagons over the frozen Vistula River... The city was quiet, the people ashen, despondent. On the other side of the river, on the left bank, the King's Castle had already been burned during the bomb raids as well as many other buildings downtown."

The ever-present threat of deportation still loomed and during the early days of the war, an estimated 2,000,000 healthy young Poles were sent to Germany for slave labour, where they were forced to wear a letter 'P' on their arms. German citizens were forbidden from showing these prisoners any kindness, on pain of imprisonment. Some 30,000 children were also seized – many of them plucked from their mother's arms – and sent away for forcible

'Germanisation'. In the face of such evil, the only choices people faced was to run, hide or fight. It was clear from the outset that Artur and Zula were not the types to hide or flee. Determined to do something to help in the battle against the invaders, Artur joined the resistance first, in November 1939, the third month of the war. He enlisted in one of the many illegal military groups that were initially banded together as the Union of Armed Struggle, but which later became known as the Home Army. Because of his status and position, he was given a position in the quartermaster's office of the headquarters of Home Army Warsaw-Downtown group from where he helped organise hidden magazines of arms, ammunition and other equipment.

Zula wasn't prepared to stand idle either and – thanks to her excellent languages – she was appointed aide-de-camp to Colonel Hieronim Suszczyński of the Home Army Warsaw-Białowieża district with a remit for 'special tasks'. This involved posing as a German officer's widow and travelling on false documents to and from northern Poland – freshly incorporated into Germany – to connect with newly formed resistance cells. History doesn't record what Artur thought of his wife risking her life in this way, but he would have had long experience of Zula doing exactly what Zula wanted to do. He was probably also grateful that after her success in shooting competitions in Mława she at least knew how to handle a weapon.

Throughout their time in the Polish underground, the couple never worked together, complying with the Home Army policy that family members be assigned separately to avoid knowing anything about the other's work should either be captured. "What you do not know, you will not reveal even under torture." Nor were they allowed to perform more than one function each within the Home Army, as every mission carried a high enough risk on its own. Zula and Artur were given secret codenames that not even the other was supposed to have known. "One time Mummy couldn't find Daddy for two weeks and was running around Warsaw looking for him as 'the Painter', not knowing that his name had been changed to 'the Bald Man' who was someone she'd heard of but had no idea she was sleeping with every night."

With poor communication and so many refugees in the city, resistance took many forms – collective and individual, armed and passive – and there were constantly shifting alliances between groups. Members ranged from bankers and socialites like Artur and Zula, to miners, teachers, bakers, and soldiers. There were men, women, teenagers and children all determined to prove their courage. Those who knew each other from their hometowns helped each other, and the refugees from Mława were no exception. One of the people who became pivotal to the Home Army operations was a Catholic named Tadeusz Śliwczyński. Before the Nazi invasion, he'd worked in the Revenue Office in Mława, which is where Artur had first met him. Coincidentally, Ella was friendly with his daughter Lala.

Having fled Mława for Warsaw, Tadeusz found a job in the city tax office and then worked out of the courthouse on the edge of what was to become the ghetto. There, he became the Home Army's best forger of documents, thanks to his unique access to the forms required for every Nazi *Kennkarte* (or ID card) that allowed a citizen to move freely under occupation. Secretly, he was able to create false *Kennkartes* using not fictional names – as was common although risky if checked – but by copying information from genuine birth and death certificates instead. These came from the parish books provided by Father Dudziński, a priest from the church of St Karol Boromeusz in Powązki, who was in league with him. By ensuring that each of the names related to a person who had since died, there was never a danger of duplication and any attempts to verify them would stand up to scrutiny.

"Mama told me with much admiration that Śliwczyński's papers were very expensive, but worth their price." Tadeusz Śliwczyński was equally helpful to Jews and other refugees at his home. He lived with his wife and son in a third-floor apartment at 11 Chałubiński Street, which became a busy meeting point for people who had fled to Warsaw from Mława and wanted news. His son Jerzy said later, "From the fourth floor one could climb to the

41

attic using other stairs, and from the attic one could easily get to the attics of adjacent buildings and then, using another staircase, leave through the building at Aleje Jerozolimskie, which was crucial in case of a police search... We were also receiving visits of Jews from Mława – in most cases Father's friends from the junior high school including a pharmacist and a doctor... The apartment was accessible for all in need... There were days where over a dozen people were staying overnight in our kitchen, so that they could continue their journey in the morning. Amongst those with whom my father was co-operating were some well-known persons, including Artur Pieńkiewicz, head of the KKO Bank in Mława."

Artur and Zula's work was so perilous that it put their entire family at risk. The fear of that, coupled with the fact that they had no income and limited access to food, led them to believe that it would be safer for their children to live with relatives who had a farm in the country. Although the idea of their separation was painful to them in such uncertain times, the only way to get enough food to survive in Warsaw by then was to barter, smuggle or steal. At least in the countryside the children would have access to fresh milk and produce and wouldn't have to boil vegetable peelings for soup or rely on the free meals dished out by the Central Welfare Council.

So, in February 1940 Artur escorted Jowita, Kalina and Pamaja through what was known as the 'Green Border', crossing the Narew River, taking them to those who'd agreed to care for them. This pattern continued intermittently in the coming years, with the children regularly staying on the farm or with Pamaja's relatives – Ksawery Bieńkowski and his family – who readily took them into the home. The shoemaker lived just off the market square in Mława and had returned to find it intact following the initial German bombardment. The family was only too happy to take in Jowita and Kalina after all Artur had done for their son. This was, they always said, the least they could do.

3

TWO SIDES OF THE WALL

In the late spring of 1940, when the mood in Warsaw had lightened somewhat (for non-Jews at least), the children and Pamaja were escorted back to the city late one night. Their new home was an apartment Artur had secured for them in a modern building in Madalińskiego Street in the Mokotów district, rented from friends who'd left to live in the countryside.

Even as a little girl, Jowita noticed how much Warsaw had changed in the months that became known as 'the phoney war', when Poland's British and French Allies took no military action and Hitler's forces were busy preparing to invade Holland and Belgium. "Mother applied make-up again. Everybody started to sew clothes or go to a tailor, repair their shoes, mend rooftops and whatever they could fix in their apartments. Many looked for space in the courtyards to keep animals such as goats or rabbits, because only goats and rabbits were not subject to requisition by the Germans. It was not permitted to keep any animals in our building, but we planted carrots and onions on the balcony in a planter, just like everyone else. In the summer many of the lawns were made into vegetable gardens, and even on the slope by the ruins of Warsaw Castle someone planted potatoes. People raised their heads and started to somehow organise their lives and ways of resistance in the reality of occupation."

At the age of six, Jowita was far too young to know that, despite this outward bravado amongst her immediate circle, life under occupation was very different for many and people were still dying in their thousands, especially the Jews. On October 12, 1940, on Yom Kippur, the Nazis officially decreed the existence of the Jewish ghetto in Warsaw and deployed slave labour to start the building of a 17-kilometre brick wall around it – a task that took almost a year. Realising that this could only be a precursor to sealing off the Jews from the rest of the city, spread widespread panic on both sides of the wall. At over three metres high and topped with barbed wire, the new barrier was heavily guarded as more and more Jews were brought in from nearby towns until there were more than 400,000 living in an area of 1.3 square miles. This massive overcrowding led to food shortages and an average of seven people to a room. Hunger, exposure, and disease took its toll on the growing population as the wall continued to hem them in. In the two years between 1940 and 1942, an estimated 83,000 died and that was before the Nazis started to deport people to the death camps.

Any false sense Jowita might have had that she and Kalina had returned to a calmer city on the Aryan side was shattered when the Germans stormed their building and threw everyone out. They announced that they planned to establish a medical sanatorium there for German soldiers wounded on the front lines. Homeless, Artur and Zula quickly found another apartment at 6 Krakowskie Przedmieście, near the famous 1828 statue of the Polish astronomer Nicolaus Copernicus. The four-storey 19th-century building was approached through a deep arched entranceway featuring heavy and ornate wrought iron gates, which were locked each night to keep the public out.

Beyond the gates there was a wide courtyard in which stood a pretty lilac tree and wooden frames for beating carpets. The family entered their part of the building via a solid wood door that led to a grand marble staircase taking them to their third-floor apartment. There was also a wooden back stairs for servants that led straight into their kitchen from the courtyard. The flat was owned by a Miss Linka, also known as Miss Paulinka, who had lived there all her life and the caretaker was a member of Artur's Home Army unit who'd arranged their accommodation. The family discovered after the war that Miss Paulinka was racially Jewish but had converted to Christianity. She lived in her own room, where she spent her time praying and rarely emerged for fear of discovery, as several of her neighbours knew that her family was Jewish. She had her own cook, an older woman by the name of Ms Nitecka, who'd worked for her parents and shared the kitchen with Pamaja.

By 1941, the city was far from calm as the Nazis continued to 'liquidate' the Polish intelligentsia – Gentiles and Jews alike – with the intention of cutting away any leaders who might rally resistance. Everyone from professors to scientists, teachers, priests, politicians, and sports figures were rounded up in what the Germans named the *A-B Aktion*. As in Mława, where Artur was still being searched for, many of the 3,500 men and women on the lists had been singled out for arrest before the invasion by German spies living in Poland. Radios and transmitting devices were banned, with severe punishments for anyone caught using them and the Nazis further ordered that all weapons had to be relinquished, and all vehicles requisitioned. Poles were only allowed to ride horses and bicycles, or travel in inferior sections of trains and trams. Bicycle rickshaws that could carry two passengers appeared on the streets, powered by enterprising young men.

The other thing that Jowita didn't know was that her father and Moshe Złotnik had already contacted each other in Warsaw. She didn't discover until much later that Moshe had access to a telephone in the ghetto after his building's exchange was accidentally included when houses on the Aryan side of the wall were reconnected. The engineers, who may have arranged this deliberately in support of those trapped behind the wall, told the Germans that the system was far too complicated to isolate a single area, so the few lines that had to remain open were closely monitored instead. Moshe remembered that Zula's parents Paweł and Jadwiga Kaliniecki lived in Saska Kępa and he found their number in a telephone book. Knowing that his conversation was almost certainly being listened to, he asked them to pass on a message to Artur that he urgently needed to speak with him, and a meeting was subsequently arranged.

Nor was Jowita then aware that – even though the Złotniks were stuck behind barbed wire and the unassailable brick wall – it was Moshe who helped Artur and Zula at first, and not the other way around. As Ella recalled, "When the war broke out all the intelligentsia were thrown out of Mława and ended up in Warsaw. The Pieńkiewicz family was without money and my father helped them a little bit."

Once the ghetto was officially sealed on November 16, 1940, its inhabitants were caught like rats in a trap. Their living space became the largest ghetto in occupied Europe, although – until the 11-mile wall around it was complete – some of its boundaries were temporary and often moved as more and more streets were excluded. The Germans strictly controlled the delivery of all goods including basic foodstuffs and whether items were allowed in or not was entirely dependent on the whim of those on duty, or by how corrupt they were. Those who had been living in the Jewish quarter before it became a ghetto were far better off than the rest, as they were in their own homes with their own belongings around them and with food they'd already stockpiled for winter and for war. Many were even able to carry on running their businesses, which gave them access to money and food. For the rest, life grew increasingly bleaker and there was great hardship and suffering as well as the terror of attack by groups of SS soldiers who took delight in publicly humiliating or brutalising Jews. Truckloads of German police or soldiers would be driven into the ghetto to fire on passers-by at random, or they would seal off a street and seize everyone they could find to send them for hard labour. Life became a daily game of chance.

Poles were not allowed to enter the ghetto and Jews could only leave in organised work groups under armed escort, or with a special permit known as an *Ausweis* that allowed them to work for the occupiers beyond the wall. Many were employed by German

46

and Polish companies that had been encouraged to set up workshops in the ghetto to take advantage of the cheap labour and qualified craftsmen. Most of the work was towards the war effort or to provide quality clothing for the German people, but the employees were paid only in thin soup or bread and their hours and conditions were brutal.

True to the Varsovian spirit, the rules about access to the ghetto were flaunted daily with people crossing in and out via tunnels, communal attics, and secret passages between basements to bring in food and medicines that were then sold on the black market. The courthouse where master forger Tadeusz Śliwczyński worked proved pivotal as the building straddled the border between the ghetto and the Aryan sector with entrances on either side, allowing people in and out. His son Jerzy said, "Jews from the ghetto could enter the court if summoned... The building at Leszno Street had another exit at Ogrodowa Street. This exit was used by many of those who never came back to the ghetto."

New ration cards were issued to every Warsaw inhabitant, based on their racial origin. All pork, grain and eggs were immediately requisitioned for Germany, and anyone found hoarding items was summarily executed. A strict ration system was implemented that allowed German citizens living across the Reich 2,613 calories a day, while non-Germans such as Poles were permitted 669 calories. Non-Aryans and Jews, who were categorised 'subhuman', were allocated just 184 calories. That equated to approximately three slices of bread daily, and this was often inedible as it was made with sawdust, flour and potatoes. Milk was almost impossible to come by, and fresh fruit and vegetables fetched astronomical prices. A kilo of sugar, which would have cost one złoty before the war, suddenly cost 65 złotys. The elderly and the very young were the first to die, and epidemics and malnutrition began to claim people of all ages.

In the face of starvation, the black market thrived and Moshe Złotnik was an astute enough businessman to capitalise on it. He was clever too. With the right papers and the money to pay bribes he knew that Artur and his wife would find it far easier to smuggle things in and out of the ghetto than any Jew. This was true of Zula especially, as women and children attracted less suspicion from the armed guards who stood day and night at the gates, checking and double-checking papers. Knowing the couple was not only willing to help but short of funds, Moshe made them an offer. Wryly, he suggested, "You know how you could be helpful to me? You can be a courier into the ghetto and take things out to sell. I am sure I know of such an adventurous woman!"

Ella said, "It was normal in the beginning in our part of the ghetto even to have a telephone to the outside and we had one. My father called up Artur and they met, and he asked if Zula wanted to be a courier into the ghetto, taking things in and out. He asked if she wanted to make money this way and she jumped at it. She was very brave and adventurous, and she decided to do it. After that she used to come to the ghetto often and once, she even stayed overnight, which was unheard of. Whenever she came into the ghetto she put on the armband of a Jew and when she walked out, she took it off and was a Christian. It became a steady thing. She was very dedicated, and she was honest. She was making a living. She was helping my father and helping herself."

To begin with, Zula almost certainly accessed the ghetto via the Lezno Street courthouse but once the Nazis tightened the noose, she would have had to use riskier routes in and out, facing the chance of possible detection time and again. One thing was for certain – in her new role as courier/smuggler/resistance worker there was never any more chance of Zula being bored.

Life in the ghetto somehow carried on despite the constant fear and the ever-present threat of humiliation, beatings or death. Many Jews tried to escape to the forbidden side with the help of friends, family and the Home Army, but heightened security and dire warnings of the consequences deterred most.

In such a climate it was almost impossible for an entire family to flee, so parents often had to take the heartbreaking decision to arrange freedom for one or more of their children, even if that meant permanent separation. In a letter from one Hungarian mother trapped in a ghetto, kept long after the war, a woman called

Zsugsi wrote to her sister-in-law, to whom she was sending her baby daughter Marika. She wrote:

With heavy heart and infinite sadness we bear this heavy burden... I don't know if you can understand what I felt when I had to part with my six-month-old angelic darling, little Marika, so her life could be spared... We are doing this because we believe that you will survive this horrific inferno and that you will take our Marika in with love... I beg the good Lord to give you strength to bear the responsibility of guardianship of our little girl, and bring her up as we would have done, that she should never lack love and attention... The fate of the letter writer and her child is unknown.

Taking in a Jewish adult or child carried enormous risks for both parties, and those in the ghetto were wary of asking anyone to help them. "My parents said most of the people in the ghetto were petrified of the Poles, many of whom claimed to be able to 'smell a Jew better than the Germans' and would readily hand them over to the Nazis for a reward," said Ella's daughter Anita. The Germans knew that a Polish Jew would be far more easily identified by a fellow Pole than by them, so they offered huge rewards to those who delivered any to the Gestapo. In a time of war, these rewards might include cash, vodka and cigarettes or they might be allowed to help themselves to the clothing, property and belongings of the family they'd denounced.

Despite this temptation, it became increasingly difficult to find any Poles who'd agree to provide food and shelter, even in exchange for a bribe of jewellery, gold or huge sums of money. Painfully aware of the severe penalties all faced, many on the Aryan side refused or insisted on taking only those with non-Jewish features – effectively condemning to death any with dark hair and eyes. Regardless of how they looked, boys were often rejected purely on the grounds of their circumcision. Even a so-called 'Jewish demeanour' could prevent someone from being saved, as a sorrowful expression or general stooping of the shoulders through years of fear or oppression could be enough to give them away.

It wasn't only physical attributes that could alert escapees to the vigilant. They had to speak Polish well and without any kind of accent, but especially not a Yiddish one. Certain expressions were identifiable too, and even the stress or intonation of a word or syllable could lead to an arrest. Jews living amongst Poles who may never have drunk alcohol before were suddenly expected to imbibe freely with their Polish counterparts for fear of standing out. Similarly, they could only eat whatever food was on offer or starve, so all thoughts of keeping kosher had to be abandoned, which often felt like a betrayal of their faith. Perhaps most difficult of all, whenever they were in company they had to agree with anyone who complained about the Jews.

If the Nazis were alerted to any escapees or to those who'd collaborated to save people from the ghetto, they'd immediately arrest them and take them to Pawiak Prison or its sister prison for women known as *Serbia*. Both had been constructed during the time of the Tsars and were located in the heart of the ghetto between Dzielna, Ostrożna and Pawia Streets. The Gestapo used both buildings and their own headquarters on Szucha Street to interrogate their victims, often torturing them pitilessly and for several days and nights before dispatching them, barely alive, to the concentration camps of Auschwitz, Buchenwald and Ravensbrück, amongst others. Many were executed on the spot. Within five years, the Gestapo accounted for 100,000 such 'disposals' – prisoners who were either shot or sent to the camps.

Conditions in Pawiak were extreme with cold, dirty and damp cells crawling with fleas and lice. The terrified men, women and children existed on starvation rations and were regularly beaten and abused or set upon by dogs. Jews and members of the resistance were treated worst of all, and the same applied to anyone accused of aiding them. Regina Domańska, in her book *Pawiak – Martyrdom and Heroism*, quotes one of the guards: "*About 150 Jews – men, women and children – were brought to Pawiak... the next morning they were taken out. At the gate of a house at 25 Dzielna Street a single shot was fired at each of them. When they were falling, fire was set to the straw lying at the gate. Many of them could not stand the pain any longer so they stood up and started to run, resembling living torches.*

Then the execution squad soldiers would chase and finish off the running prisoners with shots."

Any prisoner suspected of being Jewish but not yet proven would be rigorously cross-examined by priests enlisted by the Gestapo to ask probing questions about the rituals and prayers that would have been second nature to a Christian. Failure to pass such a test often led straight to the execution yard. Even if an escapee answered all the questions, they'd then have to back up their stories with details of their backgrounds as well as impeccable false documents. Although forgers working for the underground created hundreds of fake *Kennkarte* for Jews and others and in varying degrees of quality, they weren't easy to come by and could cost a family their entire savings on the black market. Those lucky enough to get hold of one had to invent a new identity for themselves, with a family history and a back story that would stand up to close scrutiny. Any inconsistencies could arouse suspicion and lead to disaster. With all these factors to consider, the safest course was to find a Polish family willing to take them in as one of their own and lend them greater legitimacy.

Even if a citizen of the ghetto made it safely to the Aryan side and settled into their double life, there was still the constant fear of being found out and denounced. Blackmail was so widespread that it even led to the pejorative slang term *szmalcownik* (from *szmalc* meaning lard or fat) in reference to the blackmailer getting fat on someone else's fear. More often than not, once the blackmailer had milked an escapee dry, taking everything they had, they'd turn them into the authorities anyway in the hope of further reward.

The commanders of the Home Army and other members of the Warsaw underground let it be known that anyone found either collaborating with the Nazis or blackmailing anyone in hiding would be executed – and many were – but that didn't stop them. The rewards were too high and, for many, the temptations were too great.

Ella Złotnik who was by then 17 years old, appears to have remained unaware of all this, as she helped her mother prepare food for those relatives that were still alive.

A few soup kitchens had sprung up to feed the starving and the homeless, especially amongst the orphans, and there were many people who helped those less fortunate than themselves, organising food, clothing and shelter for the destitute. Intellectual and artistic life also continued and, in many ways, intensified as the thousands of talented musicians, artists, teachers and professionals herded into cramped quarters resolved to create entertaining distractions from the daily fear and hunger. Theatres and cafés opened, and writers created satirical plays that poked fun at ghetto life, while actors, singers and musicians performed in return for a better pair of shoes, alcohol or some cigarettes. And all the while, the comprehensive system of education ensured that no Jewish child would miss out on their curriculum, despite the Nazis. Retired professors with little to eat would give one-to-one lessons in return for half a loaf of bread or a handful of potatoes.

Ella and her friends continued her schooling in secret rooms during the day and, along with their families, attended as many of the different cultural events as they could. These included Yiddish comedies put on at makeshift theatres, free music concerts by members of the Warsaw Philharmonic, jazz nights, cabarets, choirs and lectures, all of which allowed those in the ghetto to forget the war for an hour or more. This stopped in June 1941 when there was a devastating epidemic of typhus that claimed thousands of lives and placed thousands more under quarantine trapped inside their cramped accommodation for fear of infection. The Germans insisted on regular delousing and made inhabitants strip naked in public to be sprayed with insecticides. The humiliation was unbearable for many and the number of suicides, especially amongst the elderly, soared. Nothing, it seemed, could protect the Jews of Poland from death. The bodies of those who'd succumbed to disease or despair were stripped clean of their shoes and clothing and left in the streets under sheets of newspaper weighed down by stones to be collected for the communal burial pit before they were eaten by the ghetto's rats.

On June 22, 1941, Hitler invaded Russia – to the shock of Stalin and the rest of the world – as the German military advance across the vast continent seemed unstoppable. This news at least brought a little hope to those under occupation who believed that with Russia and the Allies now against Germany, it was only a matter of time before the Nazis were defeated. All they had to do was survive a little bit longer and then they could maybe return to some semblance of how life was before the war. With the Russians pushed back out of Poland, however, the Nazis were devising even more heinous ways of annihilating Europe's Jews, making the situation for all those imprisoned in the ghettos look hopeless.

One day in August, Ella's parents told her that they had some news. "Tomorrow we have arranged for you to get out of the ghetto with a working group," her father said. "Mrs Pieńkiewicz will be waiting for you on the other side, and you must go with her for a few days." Ella knew *Pani* Pieńkiewicz not just from Mława, but from her regular visits into the ghetto to see Moshe, so she assumed this encounter probably related to some black-market business. It would have been the first time that she had ever left the ghetto since the family moved there, and yet she seemed unfazed by the news, trusting her father and assuming that his instructions were important.

The group that Ella had been assigned to leave the ghetto with was one of a daily detail selected to sweep streets, fill potholes, and clean up the parks and public places frequented by Warsaw's elite. Several of her friends had been assigned to such tasks in the past and all had returned safely. The young men and women were usually split into smaller groups on the Aryan side, and Ella would be sent to clear pathways and sweep up leaves in the Saski Garden (Saxon Garden) not far from where Zula and Artur lived. She was advised to prepare for her departure by taking a few belongings from home.

"My parents arranged everything. They just said it all of a sudden. There was no preparation. I was to walk out and somebody else was to walk in in my place. The guards didn't know us by name; they just counted heads, so the same number had to return to the ghetto in the evening." Ella was too young to understand the real reason she was being asked to leave and told Jowita later, "I did not in the least realise the meaning of this step. I was certain that this was just a simple crossing from one side of the city to another, that I would separate with my parents only for a week or two and then we would meet on your side and live somewhere where we could wait the war out... When the day came and my mother started to cry, I asked, 'Why are you crying?' I didn't expect that I was going to stay there for very long. I cannot forgive myself for not bidding her a more hearty farewell... I was so little aware of what was going on, or maybe I was pushing it away from my thoughts. I was so calm; I didn't think about it. My mother became hysterical and she was crying and saying, 'How are you going to make it in life?'"

After she had dressed for her day's work and walked out of their shared room for her rendezvous with Zula, carrying a small bag of things, Ella kissed her tearful parents goodbye, not appreciating that she might never see them again. As promised, Zula was waiting for Ella in the Saxon Garden, a brightly coloured jacket hidden in her capacious bag. As she sat on a park bench and waited nervously for the ghetto detail to arrive, a thousand thoughts must have run through her mind. She had risked so much already, but this was different. Now she was endangering not just her own life, but that of her entire family for the sake of a teenage girl she hardly knew. It was true that they had a professional and personal relationship with the Złotniks in Mława during peacetime, but they had surely crossed a line by begging her to save their daughter. It was a calculated gamble on Moshe's part. He knew that Artur and Zula were not only open-minded and decent but, as active members of the Socialist Party, they were the only Poles he could really trust. He believed that their innate humanity and sense of doing the right thing – regardless of race, nationality or religion – would almost certainly seal their agreement. He was right. Although as the moment approached, even brave Zula must have had her doubts.

In preparation for her mission, she had meticulously mapped out the routes of all those sent for duties beyond the ghetto walls. She grew to recognise the various guards, investigated her various escape routes, and planned exactly how she would free Ella from the Nazi's grip. Before she could falter or change her mind, the group of 16 young men and women from the ghetto arrived in tight formation – flanked by armed escorts as usual – and were set to work in an area that had been dug up and replanted with vegetables for the war effort. Zula spotted Ella immediately but was careful not to make eye contact with her. She watched as the soldiers marched away, leaving a solitary German guard in charge. He took up his position to watch the group tidying and sweeping. When the time felt right, she got up and strolled over to him casually, smiling broadly. Ella, not knowing how this would happen or what was expected of her, watched the exchange out of the corner of her eye. Zula quietly asked the guard to look the other way for a few minutes, in return for a large sum of money she carried with her and showed him quickly inside her purse. Even to approach him in this way was an enormous risk. It would have been immediately apparent to him that she was intending to help one or more of the Jews to escape, a crime punishable by death.

Luckily for her, the guard had already been primed and his greed won him over, so he nodded, pocketed the cash and turned away. Somebody else within the resistance would have come later to take Ella's place and return to the ghetto instead so that she could escape. With everything ready, Zula locked eyes with Ella and walked up a path that passed between a clump of large bushes. The teenager silently slipped away from her group to join her. As soon as they were hidden from view, Ella quickly did as Zula instructed and switched her drab cardigan for the brightly coloured one that she'd brought. Zula's logic was that although a gaily coloured jacket might be more noticeable during wartime, no one would think for one minute that anyone risking something so dangerous would draw attention to themselves in such a way. Zula, the expert card player, was playing a double bluff. Emerging from the other side of the bushes, she linked arms with Ella and began to laugh, engaging her in a lively conversation, waving her hands animatedly and chatting away as if they were a normal mother and daughter enjoying a summer morning walk. In truth, they barely knew each other.

As soon as they left the park, Zula hurried her young charge towards Królewska Street, from where they walked to the nearby Krakowskie Przedmieście and the Pieńkiewicz apartment where everything was prepared. There were no other children at home as Jowita and Kalina had been sent away again to spend the summer in a cottage in a village called Chylice. They knew what to expect when they returned, though, as their parents had already visited them to tell them that they would have 'another sister' soon. "They told us that a teenager named Elżbieta Zofie Zabłocka, my father's sister's daughter, would be living with us," said Jowita, who was eight years old at the time. "She had escaped from the town of Lvov in the eastern part of Poland that had been occupied by the Russians. She had become separated from her parents in the confusion and would stay with us to wait for them. We accepted this without surprise, as families separated during an escape were a common occurrence then."

Zula and Artur had not only taken a huge risk by taking in the Złotniks' daughter, but they had also defied their commanders in the Home Army by doing so. All they'd been asked to do was help her escape from the ghetto, not to keep her with them as one of their own. In normal circumstances they'd have handed her over to the organisation's Committee for Aid to the Jews who would place her with Home Army sympathisers she'd never met and who weren't directly involved in any underground activities. Depending on their circumstances, she might have had to pass herself off as a Christian, or she could have been forced to live in an attic or a cellar, behind a false wall, or in any number of hiding places.

Her friendship with Celina Złotnik at the forefront or her mind, Zula argued that an exception should be made in Ella's case and that she should remain with her and Artur instead. Fearing her commanding officer's refusal, she personally coached Ella in how to play her Aryan role to perfection. When senior operators from her division visited their apartment to consider her request, they vouched that Ella looked and acted entirely Polish, so she was allowed to stay.

When Jowita and Kalina returned from their summer playing with village children, they found a girl almost twice Jowita's age sleeping on the sofa in the living room. Her few belongings were kept in the room they shared. They accepted this too, as it was also nothing new. Their days of having their own bedrooms in their comfortable apartment in Mława were a distant memory as, since then, they'd been moved from place to place and very often expected to share a space in cramped conditions. Pamaja, too, accepted her new charge.

Ella recalled, "Auntie Zula had two little daughters and a woman taking care of them. Not a governess, more like a housekeeper. A deeply religious Catholic, she was an old maid. I didn't think she was aware of who I was at first, although later it became obvious that she did know. I came in as a cousin from the eastern part of Poland occupied by Russia. They said, 'This is our cousin's daughter who got lost on the Russian side, so we have to take her in.' That was the story for the girls and this woman, and they accepted it. They called me sister because in Polish the term for cousin is like a sister by an aunt."

Like any girl her age, Jowita was understandably jealous of her new 'sibling' and especially of the attention she received. "Ella was a pleasant and very pretty young lady; blonde with curly hair, blue-grey eyes, short nose and a creamy complexion. She was very quiet, which I now realise was because she was wary of saying something unusual or different. It was easy to like her and soon everyone got used to her presence. Only I was as jealous as hell and sulking, because Mother definitely paid more attention to her than me. I think she loved her not only as she loved us, but in a special way that a person can love an underdog; someone who is vulnerable. That's why I didn't much like Ella at the time. Mama didn't put me to sleep anymore. Instead of coming to tell us a good night story as usual, almost every evening she sat with Ella as she cried, even though she cried very quietly."

For Ella, the sudden realisation that her parents had arranged her permanent removal from the ghetto without yet planning for their own escape came as a huge shock. She was, of course, enormously grateful to 'Auntie' Zula and 'Uncle' Artur but she was also extremely lonely and afraid. As Jowita said, "She was in the eye of the cyclone – which is not its worst place – in the most rebellious amongst the European cities occupied by the Germans, in a family and environment completely devoted to conspiracy."

Ella may have been safe for now, but her heart and mind was constantly with her loved ones on the other side of the wall. There was so much for her to get used to, not least her new name Elżbieta Zabłocka, which was a typical Christian surname from the Polish nobility. Zula cleverly gave her the same initials in case she had to initial something quickly she wouldn't make a mistake, and also arranged her first name so that it could be shortened to Ella. "I got used to my name very fast because I knew it was so important, but it hurt all the time and felt like a betrayal. I also had to learn the Catholic religion. Auntie Zula gave me this catechism – a book with all the rules. We lived on the street where there was a very famous church – the Church of the Sacred Cross. And the maid who was taking care of the girls would take me to church every Sunday. They insisted that I go with them, but Zula said, 'It's up to her – she's a big girl. She can make her own decision whether she wants to go.'"

Ella found it difficult to sit in a Christian house of worship that featured a large figure of Jesus Christ pointing the way, although she did try. "Once in a while I did go to church and sat there trying to connect with another god, but it didn't work for me. I felt like a traitor. I observed enough to know what to do. I just went in and watched other people. They were kneeling and praying and most of the time I looked around jealous that they had it so good and how lucky they were to be able to go to church and feel relaxed. I thought how good it would be if I could be one of them. I thought maybe I might make a connection with God there, but it didn't work so I only went a few times, for appearance's sake."

Zula and Artur both had their own quiet faith and usually only went to church at Easter and Christmas, so Ella's decision not to attend church services only made Jowita and Kalina more resentful of the girl they called sister. They hated that she was allowed to stay home while they had to sit on unforgiving wooden benches for an hour listening to incomprehensible Latin. "The sisters were so jealous because I didn't to go to church and they were angry with their mother because she was always nicer to me."

As Artur and Zula carried on with their underground activities, sometimes disappearing for days, the rest of the family tried to lead as normal a life as possible. They never knew where the adults had gone, and nobody ever asked. Ella helped with the household chores and – under Pamaja's tutelage – continued her studies with Jowita and Kalina, according to the pre-war curriculum. The family had very few textbooks, as Artur and Zula's beautiful library containing all those books they had lovingly collected and willingly shared with the Złotniks, had been lost. They'd trusted the bank's janitor to keep everything safe in Mława but within days of the German invasion he'd stripped their apartment of all its belongings, none of which they would ever see again. Using some of their paltry wages from the Home Army and money made from Zula's smuggling activities, she and Artur decided to buy some textbooks for Ella, and also instructed Pamaja to do the same, even though they'd sworn they wouldn't start another library until the end of the war. They went to one of the numerous roadside stalls where desperate people sold the last of their belongings – anything from Persian rugs to sewing machines, musical instruments to watches.

"My parents recognised one of the sellers as an older professor from Warsaw University who'd become destitute," Jowita said. "People sold everything off and there were more and more stalls since nothing was manufactured and hardly anybody had a job. They also exchanged clothing, undergarments, linens, shoes, kitchenware, fur coats and other expensive accessories, but also ragged clothing, all sorts of tools for various jobs – one could buy everything. Apparently, on the big market on Kerceli Square (the so-called *Kercelak*), one could even buy arms."

Whenever she was alone with her books, Ella found that she far preferred the solitude and especially no longer having to pretend she was someone else. Those were her favourite times. The constant subterfuge and need for vigilance was something she had never known and it weighed heavily on her. She began to worry more and more about her parents and brother in the ghetto, where she'd heard that the vermin were swarming, and decaying bodies were littering the streets. She knew that the inhabitants mostly lived from hand to mouth, and were still in daily fear of being snatched, shot or catching typhus. She was also concerned about the risks Zula had taken to save her. She knew that being exposed as a Jew would be catastrophic for the entire Pieńkiewicz family, at whose address she was now officially registered. The slightest slip on her part could cost not only her life but the lives of Zula, Artur and their two young daughters. The burden on her young shoulders was enormous.

"Very often before this people had told me I didn't look Jewish. Later on when I talked to Zula about her taking me, I asked her, 'Why me?' She replied, 'Because you had perfect looks and your Polish was excellent.'" Ella said that Zula had explained to her that she'd had several discussions with her parents about taking her out of the ghetto, and it was when they reminded her how Aryan Ella looked that Zula finally relented and said she would take her.

She added, "The only thing Zula instructed me to do every time I walked out on the streets or went to the tram – especially in summertime – was to wear sunglasses. When I asked her why, she told me, 'Nothing will give you away. You speak well. You look the part, but you have Jewish tragedies in your eyes. It is the one thing that will give you away.'" This use of a literary term for the sorrowful look carried by many Jews is endorsed in a book called *When Light Pierced the Darkness* by Nechama Tec, who wrote:

Tragedy and fear, so much a part of Jewish life, gave rise to depression, which was often reflected in the sadness of the eyes... the possibility of having sad eyes became an ever-present threat. Jews were known for their sad eyes. They could be recognised by then. Many were.

It was faithful Pamaja who became the mainstay of the household as Artur and Zula came and went. Pamaja carefully taught Ella the role she should play at the various Catholic feasts such as the Christmas Vigil dinner and the Easter breakfast, knowing by then how important it was for her to appear comfortable with the customs and traditions. "Watch me and do what I do, and you will be alright," she told her. She also persuaded her to take part in all the usual Catholic festivals, go to church once a month with Jowita and Kalina for appearance's sake, and to visit 'The Lord's Tombs' on Good Friday with the rest of the family. This Catholic tradition of 'walking the tombs' – touring the highly decorated graves in each of the main churchyards – dates back to the Middle Ages and was one of the few public gatherings allowed under German occupation. During the war, these decorations were often subversive and subtly anti-Nazi with barbed wire, helmets and bullet shells. The huge crowds of Poles who saw these courageous displays, Ella amongst them, were impressed and amused.

Despite the need for the utmost secrecy about everything, Ella knew from the beginning that Zula was in the resistance. "She worked for the *Armia Krajowa* (AK) known as the Home Army and was quite a big shot in the underground. She arranged my false papers and my *Kennkarte*. People say that the AK was not very helpful to the Jews, but I had a very different experience, a good experience. All my papers were arranged by the AK, including a false birth certificate, which I was lucky that no one ever checked. When I went to register my *Kennkarte* there was a lot of anticipation, not knowing what was going to happen and whether they would find out that I had false papers and arrest me right there. It was easy for them to check and find that the birth certificate wasn't real because it was issued in Łódź, in the German part of Poland. I don't know why they didn't check it, but they didn't suspect. But I went and everything was set and ready and that was the beginning of my new identity."

Zula must have sensed Ella's loneliness from the start because she enlisted her to help with the younger girls, asking her to take them out on finer days so that they could all get some fresh air. "Ella used to take us to a park on the so-called Royal Route and allow us to play on the bronze statue of a reclining woman," remembered Jowita. "I still have a photograph she took of us sitting there. She was always so kind." Zula also took Ella aside and warned her not to try to contact anyone she might know in Warsaw, for fear of being informed on.

"She told me to be very careful and gave me many instructions – to stay away from the Jews, not to make eye contact, and cover my eyes as before. She taught me a lot about people. She trusted nobody at that point. She had close women friends who used to come on Sunday at noon to play bridge, especially one widow from Mława that I knew, but she didn't trust even her. On Sunday morning, she would say to me, 'People are coming to play bridge, so I suggest you conveniently disappear for the rest of the day.'"

Despite the warnings, the temptation not to see those she knew became too much for Ella. She was friends with Lala Śliwczyński, whose father Tadeusz forged documents. Ella said of Lala, "I had a friend from Mława but not Jewish, even though Jews and Christians did not mingle much, and we went to different schools. Somehow, I got in touch with her, but Zula did not like it. She didn't trust her. She feared they might be a little antisemitic, but I liked to go, and this young lady became a very close friend of mine. Her brother was three years older working for the underground also at the time and used to come to parties at her house. I liked them very much."

Her best friend at school in Mława was Marysia Edelman, a Jewish girl who was also pretending to be Catholic and living with two sisters in Warsaw. Ella knew where she lived and went to see her too. "I wanted to feel comfortable with myself for a change and feel relaxed, so I went. I told Auntie Zula and she practically forbade me from going again. She was very straight with me. 'You not only endanger your life, but you endanger my life and that of my family.' She didn't tell me she was working for the AK, but I knew. I also knew that she wasn't even permitted to have me in the house because being a member of the underground meant that she wasn't allowed to take any extra risks. I saw my friend very seldom after that – once in a while when I could – and I always felt very guilty about it."

Ella's feelings were entirely natural for the many 'hidden children' whose lives depended on the kindness and courage of strangers. Living in an unfamiliar and potentially fatal world, they often discovered that their safe havens weren't very safe at all but, as one put it, "a violent sea of constant uncertainty and fear." Those who were living a lie day in day out suffered not only the loss of loved ones and of their own identity, but they also endured anger at the injustice of their situation and spent much of the war feeling confused, frightened and alone – all emotions that they were unable to express. The enormous psychological impact had a profound and lasting effect on many of those who escaped the ghetto and were forced to hide in plain sight. Were they Catholic or Jewish? How could they possibly complain about their lot when their families were enduring unspeakable horrors behind the wall?

Their chameleon existence meant that they had to learn how to blend in with everyone around them, never stand out, and shut down all their feelings in order to survive. For Ella and thousands like her, displaced, and beleaguered with little sense of who they were and where they belonged, it was easier to remain silent and introverted, fearful of everyone and everything, and afraid of becoming a burden to the point that they became almost frozen in time emotionally – trapped behind their own inner wall.

4

RESISTANCE

Artur and Zula seemed fearless to Ella and continued to risk their lives almost daily in other ways for the Home Army, from whom they received their irregular salary. Their chief income, however, continued to be from Zula's sideline in smuggling when she travelled to Krakow, Mława and other towns and cities with food and grain that she sold before making important connections with other resistance groups.

She passed instructions from Warsaw, carried false documents, and collected intelligence regarding troop movements. On one trip she even returned with secret photographs of parts of the new V1 and V2 missiles salvaged after testing from the fields by diligent peasants. Much of this information was passed on to the Allies in London, where it was recently admitted that more than 70 per cent of all intelligence regarding the German military movements in the Eastern front were received from the Polish Home Army.

To achieve all this, Zula followed routes well trodden by fellow smugglers, many of whom were former burglars and petty criminals who'd adapted their activities to their wartime circumstances and now boasted that they were smuggling for the 'Motherland'. Sometimes alone and often in their company, Zula regularly took a train from Warsaw to the Masovian towns she knew well, beyond the border marked by the River Narew and into the annexed part of Poland and the German General Governorate. There she waited for nightfall. Overnight, she had to avoid the vigilant German border patrols and then cross the river by boat or by walking across the ice in the winter, before hiding in a farm building until she could catch the northbound train that passed through Mława. Under the guise of a German officer's widow, she sat in the *Nur für Deutsche* carriage, where she risked being discovered daily. Her comrades-in-crime, professional crooks who were also travelling on false papers, were taken aback by this well-dressed, well-spoken woman who stood out from the rest. They began to jokingly refer to her as 'Madam', or 'little lady' and noticed that she carried very little contraband by comparison to the gold and other valuables they were weighed down with.

One night, when several of them were hiding in the long grass waiting for a border patrol to pass, one of them introduced himself as Felis and offered Zula a few tips. "Madam runs like this for free?" he said, incredulous. "A bigger cargo would be better. Even if they requisition your lard or onions during an inspection on the train, they won't search for anything more important." He explained that German train car inspectors frequently took bribes and preferred to confiscate some of the merchandise for themselves rather than make an arrest, because this provided them with a steady income.

Thanks to this friendly advice, Zula upped her game. As Jowita recalled, "On each trip she took a rucksack of chosen merchandise, things missing at that time in the Reich, and then she took back things one could not obtain in Warsaw – just like every smuggler. And like every smuggler she made money on the price difference, which was significant." She was well aware that her activities carried heavy penalties, including being sent to a concentration camp, but as almost everything was forbidden and she and so many others faced the camps or death for far lesser crimes, it was a risk she was prepared to take.

Her new smuggler friends proved to be key to her survival and they saved her life on more than one occasion. The first time was when they were confronted by a border patrol that opened fire on them in the dark. At the last minute, she was pulled into a hiding place by the roadside that she was unaware of and only they knew about. On the second occasion, she almost died. They were crossing the river in a boat one bitter winter's night when a German spotlight suddenly flicked on from the opposite bank and they again came under fire. The men all jumped into the icy water and pulled Zula in with them. By the time she returned home to Warsaw after a two-hour ride in a freezing cold train she was frozen, her clothes stiff with ice. Semi-conscious, she walked into the apartment, smiled at her shocked family, and passed out.

Jowita said, "Everybody was terrified and wanted to cut off her clothes, but luckily Grandpa was visiting us that day. He firmly asked us to leave her alone and allow him to use an old, tested Siberian method. He told us to put an oilcloth on the sofa, covered in many blankets, and then laid her on top in all her frozen clothes including her coat and hat, except her shoes, and covered her carefully with warm covers. He had her drink a big glass of some infusion made of herbs and strong vodka and wait until she melted the ice herself. We waited in horror. Mother fell asleep. From white she became pink, then completely red, until at last the ice had melted and the covers became wet. Then Father carried her to the bathroom. Pamaja undressed her, bathed her, towelled her dry and put her in bed. Mother went to sleep again and got up after a few hours as if nothing had happened. She didn't even cough."

Dramatic events like this were fortunately rare and life for Ella and the two young girls followed the same general routine. Every day was undoubtedly a struggle with little money or food, coping with the cold and hunger, never knowing who might come knocking at their door to arrest them, or if one of their loved ones might not return home, but at least they had a roof over their heads and food on the table. They had electricity too, albeit sporadically as the Germans allowed it to different properties at different hours and on different days. Having drawn the blackout blinds made of sturdy black paper, making sure that no light could escape, the family would sit together by the light of two candles or a hissing carbide lamp.

Coal was almost impossible to obtain, and they never had enough to light all the fires in the apartment, only the large, tiled stove in the living room next to which Ella slept, so everyone would gather around it at night. She and Jowita were often put to work darning socks and mending stockings, something Ella was good at, while Kalina unravelled old woollen garments for Pamaja to knit new ones. They might play cards or knit or make cigarettes to sell. If Artur was home, he would usually write or play Solitaire while Zula knitted to calm herself. When she grew bored, she'd select a book to read from, usually something humorous by Rudyard Kipling, Jack London, Alexandre Dumas or a Polish writer, and occasionally Ms Nitecka, the cook, would join them to listen.

On any given night there could be some kind of disturbance that would shatter this contented domestic scene. Jowita remembered one such evening: "In the courtyard we heard two fast series of gunshots, breaking glass and a loud conversation. Father got up calmly, went to our bedroom and closed the door behind so the light wasn't visible from the courtyard when he lifted the blinds. He checked what happened. It turned out the police patrol shot at our neighbour's windows across the courtyard. It was to be expected. A few times already Mr Wróbel, the caretaker responsible for keeping order, as well as other neighbours had drawn attention to the fact that the blinds were poorly attached, and the light was visible from afar. Pamaja asked whether anybody was shot. Father said no, because any shots from the courtyard into the fourth-storey window must have hit the ceiling and anyway no one was screaming. Let's hope that the police won't harass Mr Wróbel, he is such a nice and helpful man."

On summer nights or when Artur and Zula were out, the time was spent differently. Pamaja would hold classes for the girls in the dining room or Ella would do her homework in the bedroom. She was a bright student and, after a while, Pamaja admitted that she couldn't teach her anymore so Zula decided that Ella should be matriculated in order that she could go to university when the war was over. They were still convinced that day would come soon.

Ella certainly hoped so, as it was becoming almost impossible to imagine her parents and brother ever getting out of the ghetto. In November 1941, Ludwig Fischer, governor of the district of Warsaw, introduced the death penalty for anyone caught leaving the ghetto and also for any Poles found to be helping Jews to do so. This sentence was carried out on the spot and without any trial, Poles and Jews shot side-by-side. A month later, soon after the Japanese attack on Pearl Harbor that triggered the United States declaring war on Axis forces, the Governor-General of Poland, Hans Frank, issued an official edict on the matter:

Jews who, without authorisation, leave the residential district to which they have been assigned will be punished by death. The same punishment applies to persons who knowingly provide hiding places for such Jews. Abettors and accomplices will be punished in the same way as the perpetrator, and attempted act in the same way as an accomplished one. In less serious cases the sentence may involve penal servitude or imprisonment.

Executions became more frequent and in one incident, eight Jews, including six women, were publicly murdered for escaping from the ghetto. Under the German rule of collective responsibility, all family members were punished for one person's transgression. The Nazis often rounded up a random group of Jews and shot them too, even if they had no connection with the escapee. Yet still people from both sides risked everything to help free those who were dying in their thousands. As more people attempted to flee, the Nazis repeatedly foiled them by ordering unexpected guard changes and random round-ups, known as *łapankas* by the Poles.

Terrified of the consequences, the numbers of escapees and ghetto beggars on the streets dwindled. Only the smallest children were able to travel to and from the ghetto regularly, capitalising on their size to slip through the narrowest of gaps. The sight of this army of child smugglers on the streets was pitiful. Emaciated waifs in ragged clothing, filthy, barefoot and permanently hungry, were often supporting entire families. Begging openly, these ghostly figures held out scrawny hands for food or anything of value. Some of them sang in thin voices, hoping for payment. Ella had to cross the street or look away rather than face them.

Astonishingly, on both sides of the wall life in Warsaw went on. The spirit of resistance is what kept most of its citizens going, along with rebellious anti-German graffiti on the ruined buildings, popular songs, satirical poems and small acts of individual defiance. Even though the Nazis had liquidated Polish schools and all education was officially banned for Poles, Zula registered Ella as her sister-in-law's daughter with the high school she herself had graduated from in 1927. The *pensja* run by headmistress Mrs Janina Tymińska continued to operate in just the same way as those Jewish schools Ella had attended in the ghetto, with classes in the *tajne komplety* (secret sets) education network organised by the Home Army and by the Polish government in exile in London. The *Tajna Organizacja Nauczycielska, TON,* or Secret Teaching Organisation was set up by those scholars who had survived the *A-B Aktion* and were determined to ensure the post-war reconstruction of Poland and to counter the Nazi determination to eradicate Polish culture. Between them, they are estimated to have taught over a million children. Some 10,000 students received master's degrees at secret universities and 18,000 graduated from high school.

Small groups of five or six pupils would meet at different locations and at different times every day, often in the mornings, so as not to arouse suspicion or alert unsympathetic neighbours. If they had to carry forbidden notes or textbooks – always risky in case they were stopped and searched – they hid them under their clothes or tied them around their waists with belts. "I carried a book of the history of Poland under my blouse and was always so afraid that it would drop out," said Jowita, "but children weren't especially looked for."

Pamaja gave Ella a small shopping bag with a hidden compartment for hers, and the rest of the bag she filled with craft materials or personal female items that would deter a soldier from delving further. Most of those involved in the street searches were looking for either underground literature or contraband food such as meat, bread, butter, honey, or fat. The punishment in either case could be a death sentence or transportation to a concentration camp. The Nazis took no interest in younger children like Jowita and Kalina, who also enrolled in the *komplety* system. Ella, being over the age of 15 from which time one had to carry ID, was far more likely to be stopped.

In her illegal classes Ella was taught Polish, history, French, chemistry, Latin, biology, physics and maths. Dolls and wool or fabrics were strewn around each classroom under which to hide books if someone burst in, and someone would be assigned to keep watch. "We had classes in a different apartment each time, and once a week it was in our apartment," she said. "We studied three subjects in four hours in one day. One teacher came for an hour, and another for an hour-and-a-half and, then the next. They worked it out this way. A priest used to come once a week and teach religion."

Zula was terrified that Ella might give herself away in the religious classes if she was asked any questions, so she told the priest that Ella was a Protestant, not Catholic, and free of religion. She claimed she'd be taking religious instruction from a Protestant minister instead. Ella had another reason to be wary in her classes, after she concluded that there was another hidden Jew amongst her classmates. "I knew that she was Jewish and I'm sure that she knew I was Jewish without telling each other. I don't know how; I knew I just felt it. The same thing in her eyes as in mine – plus she had a similar arrangement to me. There were no parents, just an aunt and uncle. And she was extremely bright."

Knowing the risks, Ella never let on to the other girl that she was Jewish and neither did she. It was a bittersweet time for her, as she longed to be amongst her own again. "I still craved to be with my friends and be myself. Not to play roles anymore. That would have been so refreshing. Even though Zula was everything for me, I felt on my own. As brave as she was, though, I didn't complain about anything. She was my mentor. I learned everything from her. She was extremely intelligent person, very understanding and very brave."

To continue to pass herself off as a normal Polish girl, Ella walked around town as freely as the occupation allowed, trying to ignore the constant presence of the Germans and the local police who collaborated with them. Her looks and flawless Polish meant that she didn't stand out from the hundreds of other Warsaw girls. Wherever she went, though, she had to remain constantly on alert. All strangers, no matter what age, were to be regarded with suspicion. Even if she did make friends, she felt safe with, how should she react if one of them said something that offended her about the Jews?

One day, after a pleasant afternoon studying Latin and French with a girlfriend called Danuta, it was decided that she would stay for supper and a sleepover as it was too late for her to get home before curfew. The two girls slept in the same bed and, after extinguishing the candles, Danuta began to ask Ella questions about her life in Lvov. Feeling endangered, Ella said she didn't feel like talking about it and wanted to go to sleep, at which point Danuta unexpectedly started to rail against her grandmother's Jewish neighbours. "They were mean, stingy crooks," she declared. "You have no idea what mean people they were. I hate Jews. I know them well; they won't cheat me. I would feel a Jew through an oak board!"

When she returned home later, Zula asked how her study night had gone. Ella told Zula sadly, "I learned many things but not French or Latin." She then relayed everything that Danuta had said. Halfway through her sad story Zula interjected with a question: "And what did you wear?" Without thinking, Ella replied, "Nightgowns," and they both erupted into laughter. Jowita said, "As always, when it was necessary to relieve the tension, Mother found a way to ridicule the situation." Needless to say, Ella never stayed with Danuta again and Zula immediately asked Artur, who knew Lvov, to improve Ella's knowledge of the town Lvov with much clearer instructions about everyday life there, which she had to learn by heart.

As part of their guise as good Polish citizens, Artur and Zula worked for the *Złoty Ul* or Golden Beehive Theatre, a venue for satirical cabaret, at Nowy Świat 19 in Warsaw, one of the few theatres permitted by the Germans. A family friend, an actor by the name of Krakowinski also worked there and his brother was the director of the theatre. Through them, Artur secured a job in the basement as a cloakroom attendant taking coats and hats, which gave him an *Ausweis* that allowed him to be out after curfew and prevented him from being sent to Germany for slave labour. It didn't pay well but he earned a bit extra through tips. Zula, who listed her occupation on her German identity papers as a *Schriftsteller* or writer, penned plays, wrote books, and worked with the actors and directors, occasionally appearing in her own shows. These were the couple's official occupations, but they also had hidden benefits because the theatre became one of the places where members of the underground met to exchange information and smuggled goods.

The cloakroom proved especially useful for relaying messages and passing contraband without raising suspicions, and the busy theatre provided the perfect cover for clandestine meetings and other illegal activities. Vital documents were swapped including false identity papers, letters, maps and reports detailing information about German movements, as well as weapons and orders. Jowita said, "We knew nothing about this aspect of their work in the theatre, but each night, my parents brought home a bag of metal cloakroom tickets, which my sister and I had to organise in numerical order and thread on strings so they could be put onto hangers the next day. Normally the cloakroom attendant puts the ticket back onto its hook right after giving the coat back to a spectator, but this slows them down which made people very nervous in view of the upcoming curfew. Ella sometimes helped us organise the tickets, unless she had other activities, but in general she was excused from it. 'Ella must study and not play with numbers,' we were told."

There were other means of resistance at the Golden Beehive too. Code words were written into the dialogue of performances that passed secret messages to those sitting in the audience, waiting for news. One of those actors was Zbigniew Rakowiecki, a handsome young man in his late twenties, who was a friend to Zula – along with his wife Karolina. Known as 'the actor with the radiant smile' he was a committed member of the Home Army and had the codename Leszek. In August 1944, he was captured and murdered by the SS and buried in a mass grave.

The basement of the Golden Beehive where they all worked had other secrets too – a hidden back exit that joined it to the cellar of a ruined cinema that had been bombed in the German air attack in 1939 and was abandoned. This is where the Home Army kept many of their weapons in a secret arsenal, which was under Artur's control as deputy to the quartermaster of his Home Army Downtown division. The importance of this storage facility was vital to the Home Army and those in charge needed to be careful in choosing who worked at the theatre and who knew about its secrets. Ella was one person Zula knew she would trust so she secured papers for her to work in the theatre as a cloakroom attendant as well. The documents she was given that permitted her to work had the double effect of rendering her exempt from the latest round-ups of beautiful young Polish women who were being taken in their hundreds to service German soldiers.

Experienced in the art of subterfuge, Zula carefully coached her protégée how to behave in public and directed her what to say if she was ever confronted or challenged. The Golden Beehive also had a telephone, so it was there that Ella was able to speak to her father Moshe once a week or so, but the news was not good. Conditions in the ghetto were getting worse. In March 1942 came the shocking announcement that although the ghetto was already horribly overcrowded, an area known as the Small Ghetto, south-east of Chlodna, would be closed and everyone who lived there would be forced to cross the specially built wooden footbridge and relocate to the Big Ghetto further north. This created not only a frenzied trade in apartments, for which money or tradeable goods were desperately needed, but also widespread panic that led to a rush of attempted escapes, murders and suicides. The Gestapo capitalised on the frenzy in their hunt for hidden Jews.

One day, the peace of the Pieńkiewicz home was disrupted by the unexpected arrival on the kitchen stairs of a hysterical, rather strange-looking woman and her near catatonic three-year-old son Stanislav, known as Staś. When asked by the cook who she was, the woman pushed past her and ran into the dining room where Pamaja was giving the children a class. Screaming, she demanded to see 'Mrs Zula' immediately. Jowita said, "Mother just took one glance, said something to Pamaja, who left to the kitchen and told us to take little Staś to our room to play with. He sat down on a chair and froze stiff as a puppet. Beyond the door we heard his mother saying something to our mother so fast that I could not understand much. Then she started running around and screaming that she couldn't take it any longer, that she would kill herself and the child." The children discovered later that the Jewish lady was Mrs Rywka Szaniecka, known as Irena, and she had fled from her apartment block with her son. She was hysterical and, eventually, Zula took control of the situation and shouted at her to sit down and explain exactly what had happened.

Taking a breath, their visitor said that the Germans had come looking for her husband Alter, just before the curfew. Her neighbours heard the commotion and they helped her. They placed Staś in the elevator, put up a sign that it was out of order, and sent it to the top floor. They quickly dressed his mother as a maid and told her to start washing the stairs. The Germans marched past her obliviously, searched her apartment for over an hour and then left, ordering everybody to stay inside because of the curfew. Everyone knew that there was a chance that they might come back, as they often did. While everyone hid in their apartments and Mrs Irena took refuge in a neighbour's flat, her son Stanislav remained alone in the elevator all night until she could find out where he'd been secreted and rescue him.

Traumatised by the time he reached the Pieńkiewicz apartment, Staś couldn't move or speak and when Jowita and Kalina tried to engage him in a game, he slumped in his chair, semi-conscious. Panicking, they cried out and Zula and his mother ran to the room and tried to comfort him, which wasn't easy. "His whitened fingers

74

were gripping the sides of the chair so tightly it was impossible to pry them open," Jowita said. "Luckily, Pamaja came in with hot herbal infusion. She told Mrs Irena to put one hand on her son's head, and with the second slowly massage his back while singing something calming like a lullaby. After a long while, Staś relaxed but still grasped his mother very tightly. Pamaja and our mother decided that now Mrs Irena should take Staś to the bathroom, give him a bath in a big washing-up bowl, dress him in my younger sister's gown and put him to sleep on the sofa in the office, where she should lie next to him and make sure he was quiet. Mrs Irena agreed and soon after having drunk Pamaja's herbs, they both fell asleep."

The family was wealthy and had already asked Zula and Artur to help them secure false papers for their family. Now they needed papers for themselves, so that they could remain safely on the Aryan side. Zula not only helped them with that, but she also eventually found a new safehouse for mother and child to hide in until they'd recovered from their ordeal. It isn't clear whether Ella witnessed this event in person, but she was certainly aware of them staying in their apartment until they could be found somewhere and gave a brief testimony about it later.

Their story about the Gestapo hunting down Jews must have made her even more fearful of her future and distressed about the fate of her parents and brother in the ghetto. It was becoming clearer to everyone that the Nazis planned to murder an entire race. What wasn't yet known was that after the Wannsee Conference near Berlin in January 1942, Hitler's 'Final Solution' had been secretly set in motion. The Germans began to open their new killing centres specifically designed for the extermination of the Jews. In Poland this was innocuously named Operation Reinhard.

On June 26, 1942, the BBC in London issued a broadcast, based on a detailed report by Szmul Zygielbojm, a member of the Polish government in exile who'd used a clandestine network of informants across Poland to glean information and had then smuggled the microfilm to London hidden inside a key. The BBC report stated:

According to the data obtained so far, the Germans have killed a total of around 700,000 Polish Jews. Everything indicates that the Germans intend to make good Hitler's announcement that if they were to lose the war, all the Jews would be murdered within five minutes of its end. We steadfastly believe that the Germans will be held to account for these crimes. But this is not sufficient consolation for the Jews doomed to death. It is our belief that the government of his Royal Highness and the Allied governments will find retaliation measures that will force the Germans to halt their bloody work.

This announcement was heard and repeated around the world and reproduced in the underground press along with claims that the Nazis were committing 'industrialised murder' and gassing Jews daily. Still no help arrived.

By the summer of 1942, Adam Czerniaków, the head of the *Judenrat* in Warsaw, was ordered to deliver 6,000 Jews per day for 'resettlement in the east' until all from the ghetto had been deported. He knew only that this meant death although it is unclear if he knew the manner or the location – asphyxiation in the gas chambers of the Treblinka extermination camp, 80 kilometres north-east of Warsaw. Posters were put up all over the ghetto ordering those selected for 'labour' to report to the *Umschlagplatz* – the huge holding area next to the railway station – for transportation, on pain of death. As part of the so-called *Grossaktion Warschau,* incentives of free food were offered that were too tempting for many of those who chose to go willingly. Extra bread, sugar, jam and margarine were promised along with the chance to escape the misery of the ghetto for somewhere that might be less crowded and give people the chance to earn a living. Hundreds lined up to go, carrying everything they could to take with them, including pots and pans, clothing and other possessions. Waving their families goodbye, they promised to write.

Rounding up those who didn't want to go voluntarily was far more of a problem and the Nazis warned Adam Czerniaków that failure to comply with their orders and provide lists of names would result in the execution of 100 hostages, including Czerniaków's wife Niunia, who would be the first to be shot. After agonising over his untenable position, on July 23, 1942, the head of the *Judenrat* swallowed a cyanide pill and died. In the note he left, he wrote:

They are demanding that I kill the children of my people with my own hands. There is nothing for me to do but die.

The Nazis quickly appointed a more compliant deputy and the deportations continued without delay. Thousands were rounded up and marched to the *Umschlagplatz* before being sent east. The only Jews who were exempt were those who had connections with the members of the *Judenrat* or who had special permits to work for the Nazi war machine in the factories outside the ghetto. To make up the Nazi quota, round-ups occurred daily, often carried out by merciless Ukrainian soldiers who were brought in especially for the task. The old, the very young and the sick were the easiest to catch. For eight weeks some 4-7,000 people a day were hunted down and captured in these *Aktions* before being shuttled to Treblinka, including many of Ella's relatives and both sets of grandparents.

Over the next nine months, the ghetto population would shrink from over 500,000 to a tenth of that through deportations or death from disease, starvation, suicide and murder. Reports at the time said,

Afterwards, the streets were littered with books, mattresses, feathers from pillows, children's toys – everything empty – everything a reminder that in five or six weeks 300,000 people had been taken away.

Another witness wrote:

In the glow of the unparalleled golden Polish autumn, there shines and sparkles a layer of snow. This snow is nothing but feathers... the disembowelled intestine of Jewish bedclothes... left here with all the other belongings, from wardrobes, chests and suitcases full of underwear and clothing to bowls, pots, plates and other household items by... hundreds of thousands of Jews evacuated to the east.

One night in the summer of 1942, Jowita heard Ella sobbing again after the lights had been turned off. Zula stayed up until very late with her and then for several nights afterwards. When the girls asked what was wrong, their mother said simply that Ella's brother Ishay had been killed.

"How did you comfort her?" Jowita asked. "What could you say?"

"Nothing, because in such instances one cannot say anything," Zula replied. "One can only be close so that the desperate person has someone to hug, so he or she knows they are not alone and has at least that what the Russians call the 'touch of a friend's elbow.'"

It wasn't until after the war that Jowita discovered that Ella's 13-year-old brother hadn't died in the ghetto or on a transport, as she'd first assumed. Unbeknownst to her and Kalina, their mother had secretly smuggled the boy out of the ghetto in the summer of 1942 as the transports east began. Although there was a doctor in Warsaw who could alter noses and even camouflage circumcisions, this would not have been sufficient for Ishay with his Yiddish accent and red hair. Instead, his parents decided that as he could never pass as a Christian on the Aryan side he needed to be taken elsewhere. They arranged for him to stay with friends in a regional ghetto where it was believed that conditions were better than those in Warsaw, where the bitter winter had claimed thousands more lives. Then Moshe contacted Artur. "Times are desperate," he told his old friend. "Please save our boy as soon as you can. Should my wife and I perish at least two children will be saved."

Ella said she 'danced with joy' at the news that her brother would be saved and prayed that her parents might follow soon. "The situation in the ghetto was very bad already and we knew the liquidation was coming, so they decided that they would try to get my little brother out. He didn't look as Christian as I did and was circumcised so was in a much more difficult situation. Zula had helped a few other people escape but she couldn't take everyone in. So my mother suggested they contact my parents' close friend, Fayvel Opatowski, and his wife, Chana, who'd lived in Mława and ran a famous Yiddish literary salon there. By then they were in the Jewish quarter of the town of Węgrów 90 kilometres from Warsaw where Chana's brother was president of the Jewish committee and they had already written to my mother the previous year, urging them to send me and Isha there. Chana, who agreed to take my brother, wrote: *The ghetto isn't enclosed so the situation isn't so bad. Perhaps we will survive these horrible times.*

The *Judenrat* that ran this ghetto had thus far managed to avoid liquidation or being subsumed into the Warsaw ghetto by bribing their German captors with gifts and cash. Diamonds, furs, gold and clothing had been paid out regularly over the years to offset further transportations, so it seemed that it was a safer place. The family promised better conditions than in the capital and assured them their daughter, who was a little bit older, would keep Ishay company until the end of the war, which everyone still believed had to end soon. As Jowita explained: "The Złotniks wanted to send Ishay there so that he could wait the war out, as it would surely end quickly. Now, when we know what this war was and what the ghettos were, it is difficult to believe in such plans, but at that time nobody would have imagined that one could plan to murder an entire nation."

The Polish people had several reasons to be hopeful. The planned Nazi invasion of Britain had been stopped by the RAF, the Russians had switched sides after Hitler breached their non-aggression pact by invading in June 1941, and Hitler's march on Moscow and siege of Stalingrad had been thwarted by brutal winter weather. In North Africa, the Nazis had failed to secure the Suez Canal or the oilfields, leaving them short of fuel, and the tide felt to be turning. "People slowly organised themselves with schemes that allowed one to somehow survive 'Until the spring!' – as the saying went. I didn't know why until then or what each coming spring was to bring, but I do remember one thing: I did not hear one person who would not be expecting a victory. People did not wonder how the war would end, but when."

As requested, Zula travelled into the Warsaw ghetto at great personal risk and took Ishay out, bundled up in clothing. She must have secured false papers for him and bribed another guard. They agreed upon the story that she was his aunt, taking him to visit his mother in Węgrów. To avoid being caught out, he would pretend to have a bad toothache, with a large scarf wrapped around his face and head to hide his hair, which had turned a rich dark red shade. "It was beautiful hair," Ella recalled wistfully. "They called it Jewish hair as only Jews had red hair. It was the same hair as my grandmother's, but she wore a headscarf so you couldn't see it." On the crowded train east Zula did the best she could to hide the boy's distinctive features from the peasant women chatting endlessly and travelling with their baskets of wares, but Ishay grew so hot with his head covered that he started sweating profusely. In exasperation, he eventually pulled everything off him and complained out loud with his heavy Yiddish accent, "Oy! It is too hot!"

The carriage immediately fell silent, and it was clear to Zula that the peasant women knew instantly that the boy was a Jew. It would have been easy for them to have reported them both to the guards for a handsome reward. Instead, they warned her to be careful and to keep him hidden, telling her, "If this is your nephew, you better return him quickly to his parents and escape to Warsaw. There you will hide more easily because you do not look like a Jew at all, but with this child it's impossible!" Another woman took a seat between Ishay and the carriage door to hide him from view of the corridor. Zula quietly thanked them and prepared to disembark.

She managed to get Ishay safely to Węgrów, but the moment she saw the Jewish quarter she doubted that conditions were any better than Warsaw. Many of the ghetto's fittest men had been forced to build the death camp at Treblinka 40 kilometres north, and had never returned. After years of paying bribes to save themselves, the remaining Jews had little left to barter with to stop them being sent there also. The *Judenrat* even ordered its police officers to raid the homes of those whom they thought might still have some valuables or gold to use as trade. Mr and Mrs Opatowski tried to reassure her that all would be well and promised to treat Ishay like their own. "We will guard him like a treasure," they told her. Pushing aside her misgivings and unable to take him back to Warsaw, Zula left him as planned, unsure if she had done the right thing.

She was right to be anxious. At dawn on Yom Kippur,

September 21, 1942, the Węgrów Jewish quarter was liquidated. German SS units along with Polish and German police, the Polish fire brigade and Ukrainian soldiers went from house to house in the mass *Aktion,* ordering the population of 9,000 people to the town square. Anyone who resisted was shot. An estimated 5,000 Jews were sent by cattle wagons to Treblinka where they perished. Almost 1,000 fled to the woods but were caught and shot. Ella said, "The safe place wasn't safe. Zula found out what had happened. They were given no warning. One morning, the Germans came in and they took them outside to the woods. They had to dig their own graves and then they killed them all." Less than 100 of the town's inhabitants survived the war. Ishay Złotnik was not amongst them.

It is not clear how and when Ella's parents learned of their only son's murder, but they did eventually receive the terrible news at a time when they were in grave risk of deportation themselves as the round-ups continued relentlessly.

Somehow, they were able to hide with their friends and neighbours in the maze of mouldy cellars beneath their building in Karmeliska Street. They shared this shelter with the Biberkraut family, including Ella's good friend Ala. Later, when the numbers of Jews dwindled still further as the trains kept coming to take people away, the street in which they lived was designated 'free' and any remaining Jews were ordered out immediately. A group of them moved into empty buildings a few streets away, including the Biberkrauts, where once again they had to live by their wits.

Descriptions about those last desperate days in the ghetto, especially during the winter, make for harrowing reading. One survivor wrote:

During the winter I was very cold; to keep warm I stayed in bed covered by whatever I could find. I was continuously hungry. Because of flour shortages the meagre bread rations that we received contained sawdust. I was dreaming of the white Kaiser rolls that I had for breakfast before the war. In the ghetto, young starving children were begging for food, dead bodies were just lying in the streets.

Another survivor, Peretz Opocynzki, said that in the desolate ghetto and against the backdrop of an abandoned city, they could hear at night the howling of the last orphaned dog – a hoarse, choked bark that sent shivers down the spine. "The dog's cry echoes like the howl of a thousand desolations. When the dog stops wailing for a moment, the ceaseless train whistles can be heard and they are no less intimidating. These are not trains bearing greetings from faraway, from the freedom of the open fields; they come, rather, from the fields of murder, from the slaughterhouse. The trains seem to howl their loneliness, even as the last dog in the ghetto is howling his."

In Moshe's few snatched telephone conversations with his daughter, he played down the gravity of their situation and assured her all was well. "There was a time when my father was ill and my parents were still in the ghetto so I was in daily contact with them on the telephone," she said. When Moshe next called, it was from the ghetto church for the converts in Warsaw, as he told her that his phone had been 'disconnected'. The more likely scenario was that he was hiding the fact that he and his wife had been forced to move. There were some 2,000 converts to Christianity who had been forced into the ghetto, all of whom had been designated Jewish under the rules of the Nuremburg Laws which only considered the faith and race of one's birth. The Church of the Nativity of the Blessed Virgin Mary, located at 32 Leszno Street, was not only the Christians' place of worship, but one of sanctuary and help for Jews. The priest was a converted Jew and it was to him that Moshe Złotnik and others turned to use the church telephone that gave them a vital lifeline to the outside.

Zula still had her business connection with Moshe, for whom it was even more important that he continue to sell for people on the black market. Once in a while she would ask Ella to collect something for her father from a building a few blocks away. This simple task made Ella feel useful and involved in his survival. On one such visit, though, she was very nearly caught. "I went up to this apartment – it was three flights up – and on the way back down a man stopped me. He wanted to grab my pocketbook (handbag). He was probably already watching me, and he knew I was picking something up. He tried to take my pocketbook, telling me, 'Give it to me, or I'll take you to the Gestapo.'

'What?' I cried. 'Why?'

'Because you're Jewish.'"

Zula had always told Ella that she had to remember that she wasn't Jewish. "Never, never admit that you are Jewish," she'd said, "because once you admit, it's finished and I'll have a tough time to disprove it."

With this in mind, Ella quickly told the man, "I'm not Jewish. You want to go to the Gestapo? OK, let's go," and she started walking very fast in that direction.

"I know who you are!" he continued shouting along the street as he hurried to catch her up. "Whatever you have you'd better give it to me." Ella just kept on walking. She knew that if she gave him her bag, she'd be admitting that she was Jewish and he would probably hand her over to Gestapo anyway. Just as she was about to cross the road to their headquarters, he suddenly pushed her into the stairwell of a building, banged her head against something, threw her to the ground, and ran off with what he wanted, leaving her empty handed. Shaken and bruised, she pulled herself to her feet and found a public telephone.

"I can't recall how I got the money to call Zula at the theatre. It was just before a performance was about to begin in which she was the star. Auntie told me to grab a horse and buggy from the city but I told her I didn't have any money and she said, 'Don't worry, we are here. We will come out and pay.' I was in shock because of the bang on my head and I stayed with them a few hours and then it was late and I had to go home."

Ella had a lucky escape and was saved by the greed of her assailant. The experience drove it home to her that there were dangers in doing even the simplest of tasks. For her and the entire family, the greatest risk when walking in the street was to be caught in any of the *Aktions* or *łapankas*, in which trucks carrying soldiers would suddenly block off both ends of a street and arrest everyone within sight – just as they had in the ghetto. Those caught in the trap would be made to stand up against a wall with their arms up or their hands in the air. They were then searched for their documents and any contraband, and – if anything untoward was found – they'd be loaded into the trucks to be sent away for slave labour or further interrogation, often never to return. Anyone who protested would be shot on the spot.

Hands tied behind their backs, thousands of innocent people were often executed by a hastily convened firing squad using machine guns. After several prisoners cried out, "*Żyj długo w Polsce!*" (Long Live Poland!) before being shot, the Germans put hoods on their later victims or stuffed their mouths with plaster to silence them. Many of the dead are now remembered in the *Tchorek* memorial plaques all over Warsaw marking the dates and locations where they were murdered.

Unless one could duck into a doorway or be taken in by a friendly stranger – many refused – anybody's *Kennkarte,* food stamps, typhus immunisation card or residence registration document could be checked and probing questions asked. Famously, one Warsaw tram driver who unwittingly drove into such a round-up and was ordered to stop and hand over all his passengers, refused to stop and sped past, screaming that his brakes weren't working. No shots were fired and he and his grateful passengers escaped.

On a winter's day, Jowita and little Kalina were on their way home from a makeshift ice rink – really just a large frozen puddle behind some buildings.

Adults poured water on one of the courtyards whenever it was very cold and we children were allowed to slide across it. There were few places to play and this was relatively safe. We had so much fun and afterwards, as Kalina and I were gaily going home, we came out of a gate onto the street and suddenly saw that the road had been closed at both ends and all the people were being loaded into trucks and sent away. It was a łapanka and we found ourselves in the crowd being forced onto the truck. I was ten and Kalina was seven or eight and we were alone.

Thankfully, they didn't want children that day – a bored soldier standing by the truck waved his hand at me and my sister, just like one waves at a dog to get out of the way, and we were let go.

Another time Jowita was walking to a class at a friend's house when she came upon a German *Aktion* in Małachowski Square, near to a building where Ella would arrive imminently for her own secret lesson. "I knew that I must save her so I ran into the agreed apartment, asked the hostess whether I could telephone my mother and once I got through, I said, 'Mama, tell Ella not to walk through Małachowski Square as it rains terribly there. It is better to walk through Krakowskie and Saxon Garden.' I heard my mother's laughter and then, next to me, my friend's mother laughed also. Mama said she understood so I calmed down." Zula later congratulated her daughter on her presence of mind but she and Ella would teasingly remind her of that 'terrible rain' in Małachowski Square.

Ella was alone on a tram reading a book when she had her next encounter with danger. She looked up and noticed a young man staring at her. Suddenly he leaned over her and whispered in her ear, "You are a Jew." Ella, not looking at him, responded, "You yourself are a Jew!" The young man turned around and jumped off at the next stop. Ella got off at the following stop and quickly returned home. Only there did she realise that her knees had gone so weak that she could hardly stand. Zula was fearful that the young man might have followed her home with a view to blackmailing her on the threat of exposing her. It was common amongst what Jowita called the 'human hyenas' to feed off the Jews. Ella was convinced that he hadn't and that he was genuinely Jewish. Her only concern was for his welfare and she wondered openly if she should have offered to help him.

Moments of light relief were few and far between in such life-threatening conditions so they were greatly appreciated when they happened. One day, Ella, Jowita and Kalina left their apartment building, which was situated almost opposite the main Polish police station, when Ella was surprised to spot a woman selling illegal bread in plain sight. Jowita remembered her as 'a cheerful crone sitting in a wide skirt covering a basket full of white wheat rolls'. She was crying out for people to hurry and buy as the Germans were coming. "The woman was not afraid. She had the same kind of quiet courage that Ella possessed and which I so admired. I, meanwhile, was trembling inside, especially when a column of policemen passed by – those who collaborated with the Germans." Inspired by the woman's audacity, people flocked to spend their *młynarkis* (occupation złotys), all of them laughing at the fact that the woman was sitting directly under a pillar on which the Germans glued their latest orders. The one immediately above her that day was an announcement that anyone caught baking or selling bread would be sent to a labour camp or executed.

Ella quickly pulled out her money and bought some rolls before hurrying home triumphantly with them and the children. Pamaja, seeing the bread and hearing Ella's story, wrung her hands and began to rebuke her for taking such a risk. When she asked her what there to was laugh about, the teenager explained and even Pamaja had to smile.

The daily privations continued with the need to search for everything they needed to live, including food and soap, underwear and shoes. One day, Zula returned from the market with a pile of clothing, including an autumn dress for Ella. Jowita remembered it well. "When our parents had left after dinner and Pamaja was teaching Kalina in our room, Ella brought the new dress to the dining room to look at it in peace. It was a sporty dress made from good quality wool, blue-grey like an airman's uniform, with four big pockets and a belt. The belt, the collar and the stitches around the pockets were of burgundy suede. In the dining room there was a large standing mirror. I sat a little behind Ella in a big armchair reading a book and I looked at the mirror and at her, how in her new dress she stood in front of it and started her examination. First, she stood straight, deep in thought. Then she turned around. Very slowly, at each moment checking in the mirror how the material lay on her body, with a different position of hands and pose. I can still see how she moved. I never saw anyone trying a dress on like she did. She looked very pretty doing this, and that is how I remember her best."

Shoes were especially hard to come by and the family was fortunate in their connection to the shoemaker Bieńkowski back in Mława, whom Zula was able to visit on her secret missions. He was able to repurpose the same shoes he had once made for her, fashioning them into smaller shoes for the children and for Ella. "Mr Bieńkowski was an artist and a master of his profession. There were no others," said Jowita. "The majority of Polish people wore slippers, sandals or shoes with a sole made of straw braids or string and sometimes even winter shoes on wooden soles. These were in a curved shape which enabled one to flex the foot. Since a lady was not supposed to leave the house without stockings even in the summer, she tinted her legs with potassium permanganate, and then with a brown or black brow pencil drew in the essential seams. It was important to look well taken care of and as someone who wouldn't be overcome by any difficulties, to walk with one's head up – and not look at the Germans. According to regulations one had to greet the Germans with a polite *Guten Morgen* but I do not remember hearing anyone in Warsaw say that."

5

IN HIDING

Like any sensitive young woman Ella could be easily upset, and one of the things that affected her especially that year was the increasing number of child beggars on the streets. Most had slipped out of the ghetto through slits in the wall or the spaces between or under buildings to beg for food to eat or take back to their starving families. Their gaunt faces and sallow skin gave Ella the clearest indication of how life was deteriorating for her parents still trapped behind the wall.

Zula warned Ella repeatedly that, no matter how sorry she felt for these pitiful urchins, she should make no contact with them or anyone else from the ghetto as someone might recognise her, which could be deadly for her and for everyone else in the family. Nevertheless, the street children increased in numbers and, with growing desperation, became more brazen. One day, two little girls who looked not much younger than Jowita and Kalina crept into the Pieńkiewicz apartment building via the wooden kitchen staircase pleading for bread and soup from the cook, Ms Nitecka. Although she was kind-hearted generally, the woman who was Miss Linka's trusty servant was an avowed antisemite who blamed the Jews for her father losing his tailoring business, which left the family destitute when she was young. To Zula's surprise, the cook gave the children what she could spare and told them to return the following day with a receptacle for some soup to take away. They did as instructed, but also arrived with two more hungry children. By the third day there were almost a dozen urchins in her kitchen – a number that could easily have attracted the unwanted attention of neighbours or passers-by. Panicking, Ms Nitecka asked Jowita to fetch her mother.

Zula told Ella to stay away from the kitchen and gathered the beggars together in the wooden stairwell before closing the door. Having appointed a teenage boy as their leader, she calmly told him that from that day on, he should divide the children into pairs and that each pair should only beg at homes where they knew they wouldn't be turned away or apprehended. She said the first two girls who'd come to beg were the only ones to come back to them, but not always at the same time of day. The boy explained that they could only come when they could. This was entirely dependent on the ghetto guards watching the exits, some of whom looked the other way while others seemed to take delight in hunting down and murdering those who trickled daily through the walls. The afternoons were best, the boy added.

The two little girls, whose names were Friede and Sara, came every day after that seeking food for their parents, grandfather and younger brother. Sometimes they also begged for clothes. They stayed longer and longer as the days grew colder, taking comfort from the warmth of the stove as they drip-fed stories of life in the ghetto. Jowita, fascinated, would wander into the kitchen, and sit down at the table to listen. Ella, still forbidden from seeing the children, often asked her about them and for news they had of life inside the ghetto. Jowita told her, "They both had small faces, narrowing into a triangular chin, what with their long noses gave them appearance of small mice. They had thick, curly hair, but other than that they were different. Sara, who was my age, had light hair and water-like grey eyes, and Friede had dark brown hair and the same small eyes. Sara's eyes constantly wandered over everything, stopping at every noise on the stairs, and then she began to shake. She calmed down only when Friede put her hand on hers. Friede was her opposite. The bright, attentive, observant girl could say a lot about life in the ghetto and Ms Nitecka constantly asked her about it, even though she did not always understand the answers as both girls spoke Polish poorly. Sometimes my mother came to listen to Frieda if she was at home and had time." Zula later told Jowita that clever, observant Friede often inadvertently gave her valuable information about the guards and the German routines that she could share with her Home Army colleagues.

The silver-haired Ms Nitecka became so attached to her 'two little mice' that she began to look forward to their daily visits. Even though she knew that thousands had died of typhus in the ghetto and feared that the girls might bring lice into the apartment, she still welcomed them warmly. She allowed them to sit close to the stove for even longer while she served them extra bowls of soup, all the while gripped by their stories. When Sara came alone one winter's day with news that Friede was suffering from a bad cold, the cook sent her away not only with food but with some herbs to treat bronchitis and some precious sugar (used only for special occasions) for the child. Before adding a piece of paper with a prescription on how to use the herbs, she gripped Sara by her chin, looked her in the eyes and said, "You must not lose this! You understand? This is for Friede, for her illness. Remember." Sara nodded and vanished.

The next day neither girl arrived and the childless old woman became so distraught that Zula had to make her some tea of dried apple peel with an extra shot of vodka. Gently, she quizzed Ms Nitecka on her change of heart about the Jews, to which the old woman replied, "I still hate them, but I don't wish them dead. That would not be Christian. And the murder the Germans do is a terrible sin! Even the children! How can you torment children? What did they do? Little Friede – smart, resourceful, works for the entire family until she got ill and one cannot even help her…" At that point, she broke down sobbing and Zula suggested that she go to church and pray for the girls. "And you think that God will listen when I pray for a Jew?" the cook asked quietly. Zula reminded her that Jesus was a Jew. "Pray for innocent children tormented by scoundrels, and God will surely listen," she advised. Ms Nitecka did as she suggested.

The wide-eyed girls with the matchstick legs came back the next day, Friede thick with cold and Sara trembling with fear. They ate their soup and accepted some to take home to their family. Jowita was in the kitchen when Friede asked to speak to 'the lady' before they left. When Jowita fetched Zula, the child stood and formally thanked her for saving them before offering the thanks of their entire family. Then she asked a favour. "She said that Sara ate the previous dinner all by herself after she returned to the ghetto, in a corner by a gate. Wide-eyed, Friede added incredulously, 'All of it! And then she came home with the empty canister and she immediately did...' (she couldn't summon the Polish word so she gestured that Sara had vomited). 'All of it! If she ever comes back again by herself, please feed her, and let her go but without the canister because one must not devour everything alone out of hunger. At home there are hungry Mama, Tata, and our small brother, who cries and cries...' The grandfather was no longer mentioned."

Jowita added, "Mama looked at Friede mesmerised and finally asked, 'How old are you?' to which the girl proudly responded, 'In January I will turn six.' My mother, whom I had not seen crying before, turned around and wept."

The girls continued to visit the family for some weeks, accepting food and German soap made from soda and green clay, but one day they didn't appear at the door as usual. For the first few days the cook kept some soup back for them but when the children still didn't come, she allowed Jowita, Ella and Kalina to eat it. After a week without a visit, she realised that her little mice were never coming back and she stopped making extra soup for them.

"It was as if they never existed," Ella said, sadly.

News of the continuing German defeat in Stalingrad in 1943 coupled with the reports that the Americans had landed in North Africa gave the Varsovians their first real glimmer of hope that the tide of war was finally turning.

What this meant, though, was that Warsaw once more came under aerial attack – this time from the Russians. As soon as the sirens sounded, every man, woman and child had to get up, collect the things they had ready at all times to take to the shelter – including gas masks – and go down to the basements of their buildings. There they prayed openly as everyone joined in. Afraid of being noticed as different, Ella would sit next to Pamaja so as not to draw attention to herself, bow her head and clasp her hands together along with everyone else to recite the devotions like a lifelong Catholic. On one particularly bad night, she heard a small boy poignantly saying his own personal prayer: "Please God, after the war, let Daddy take me to live in a city where there is no sky."

The numerous deep, old basements in Warsaw provided the only shelter against the bombs and often against arrest. Those in the know who were being chased by soldiers or fleeing an impending air attack could navigate the complex network of corridors and rooms used for storage or workshops and connected to adjacent buildings, from which they could escape. Under bombardment, residents were safe enough unless the building took a direct hit and the shelters backfilled with rubble, burying them alive.

"We were well prepared," said Jowita. "Kalina was wrapped in her quilt, and we all put on warm clothing against the cold and damp. Everyone had their own place to go to because each apartment had its own cellar for keeping coal or storing potatoes for the winter. The adults treated the bombing as a matter of fact: it was an attack on the Germans, not us, but they also feared them of course. Soviet planes bombed often and without a detailed plan, destroying a Polish district instead of a nearby German military area. In the basement, men listened to the direction of the raid and the locations of explosions, trying to guess the target of the attack. Children reacted differently – some of them treated it as an adventure while the youngest slept. One of our younger neighbours ate all the time no matter what – mostly sauerkraut – a barrel of which stood next to their space. Another asked his father to tell him a fairy tale. I read by a flashlight or a candle any book I brought, entering its world and forgetting the real one. Older women prayed, encouraging the younger to do the same."

Unusually, the family had their own early warning system of an impending air raid, as Kalina, still a toddler, would go into a kind of stiff trance each time the sirens sounded and would only return to her senses and relax her body once the raid was over and before the All Clear sounded. "Nobody knew how she was able to feel that the danger was passing," said Jowita, "but when she moved everybody started to get up and ready to leave. She reacted maybe as an animal, which feels upcoming and passing danger – in any case it did not happen that she got up too early or too late."

As a girl approaching womanhood trapped in a cellar with Catholics, Ella must have felt that her life was one big lie – she was separated from her only surviving relatives, her brother was lost, her religion denied, and her background fabricated. Each day brought the risk of discovery and, no matter how much the family that had taken her in tried to make her feel welcome, she would always be a stranger – and a danger – in their midst. Sensing her low spirits and with the plight of those in the ghetto worsening, Artur tried once again to persuade his friend Moshe Złotnik to escape with his wife and be reunited with their sorrowful daughter.

"My father once again contacted Mr Złotnik proposing him to get out of the ghetto and hide in the city, which was so much easier as Mr Złotnik had a business partner – a friend, a Pole – who was ready to hide him at his home," said Jowita. "Mr Złotnik, however, kept delaying. He answered that maybe soon, but in the meantime, he had important matters to take care of in the ghetto and he needed to stay. We do not know whether he meant financial matters, as he was trading gold and jewellery, or political." There were a growing number of anti-fascist activists in the ghetto and Jowita thinks Moshe is likely to have been involved with them. Ella was unaware of any of this; she knew only that her parents were still in the gravest danger.

There was worse news to come, though, the details of which no one was ever able to fully ascertain. One day, out of the blue, Zula picked up the telephone to hear the voice of Celina Złotnik, Ella's mother and a woman she'd not seen or spoken to in years. Their bridge nights in Mława and pleasant afternoon tea parties discussing French literature were a distant memory, as were their once comfortable lives. The books they had lovingly collected and pored over together were long gone, and each of them faced death on a daily basis. The fact that the woman who had recently lost her son dared to risk making a call to Zula at that time meant that she had something very important to say to her, and both knew that they would have to be brief for fear of eavesdroppers.

Without any prelude Celina sternly demanded, "Mrs Zula, you must promise me that you will save Ella."

Jowita, who was told of the call by her mother years later, said, "The demand was so unrealistic that Mama was speechless – she might as well have sworn that the war would end in a month. But Mrs Celina repeated the demand, or rather a command, more sternly and firmly than she had ever spoken during their years of acquaintance. Mother realised that she was – or believed that she was – in some final situation and that this was her only request.

"Without hesitating, she replied, 'I promise that I will save your daughter.' Mrs Celina responded, 'Good,' and disconnected without saying goodbye."

Within days Zula and Artur received news that Celina Złotnik had died. The story they heard from contacts in the ghetto was that she had committed suicide. She was 40 years old. Jowita said, "Mother was told that she went out onto the street leading to the ghetto gate and calmly continued walking as if she were a free person who could go where she wanted. She did not react to the order to return. She walked forward and was shot, as was to be expected."

The truth of Celina's death may never be known, but thousands of Jews unable to cope with the inhumane conditions and the persistent threat of death committed suicide in Nazi ghettos and concentration camps during the war, and through various means. Those who had contacts in the resistance acquired poison if they could, while others hung themselves, slashed their wrists, threw themselves in front of vehicles, or jumped from buildings. In camps, people often had few means to kill themselves so they threw themselves onto the electrified fences or deliberately disobeyed orders, fully understanding the consequences.

Knowing that, if true, the story of her mother's suicide would devastate Ella, Zula chose a less distressing version when she broke the news to her. She told her that her mother was working in a tavern in a German factory when soldiers came and sent the entire group on the next transport to a camp. They didn't know where. Whatever the truth, it is clear that Celina Złotnik had suffered a terrible loss in the murder of her son and the deaths of her parents – who had been sent to Treblinka along with her two brothers Gershon and Yaakov, and her parents-in-law Izak and Miriam. Losing all contact with her daughter must have felt like the ultimate loss and she was far from alone in her suffering, as this anonymous fragment of a poem saved from the Warsaw ghetto attests. It is called 'Daughter, where are you?'

> Oh, what great despair
> No, I shall nevermore see your faces
> Who will point me to your grave –
> The place where your bodies
> have come to rest forever?
> Quaking, I go round in circles,
> My soul swings from hope to despair
> My pain has no limit,
> my suffering is measureless
> I envy the dead their repose.

History doesn't record Ella's reaction to the news of her mother's death. The girls were with their grandparents and she was home alone in the apartment when Zula told her what had happened and tried to comfort her as best she could. As she'd done previously, the grieving teenager eventually had no choice but to pull herself together and busy herself with her chores and lessons.

Nobody really understood just how lonely Ella was, according to Jowita. "Her teenage life was devoid of elements of play and entertainment, but this did not differentiate her from other young girls. After their classes they could meet in cafés, as there were plenty of them in Warsaw (but they mostly had no money for this), or in each other's homes – which seldom occurred because we lived in an environment of conspirators who limited their social life to their old acquaintances. Each newly met person was unverified and could be dangerous, especially for Ella, who lived in a double conspiracy." Especially after her night spent with her antisemitic friend Danuta, she was constantly worried about meeting someone from Lvov, where she supposedly came from, who would have quickly worked out that she knew little about the place, which would in turn lead to speculation about where she'd really escaped from and what she was hiding.

It was only years later that Ella revealed that her best times were when she was home alone in the apartment after the girls and Pamaja had left for their summer in the country, and Zula and Artur were away or on missions. Once she accompanied Pamaja and the younger children to their cottage in Chylice, but she didn't like it and went back to Warsaw with Zula the next time she visited. There, she only saw Ms Nitecka for dinner and had the whole place to herself, to be herself. She could read in peace, go to the park, or study for school. As she put it, she didn't have to 'reckon' with anyone.

Jowita said later, "I wondered about that 'reckoning'. I understood that she had to be careful all the time, fearing that in this strange environment she might inadvertently hurt those who had been so kind to her by some sort of awkwardness, or reveal herself to strangers by her difference, her ignorance of their customs, or sayings they all knew. Ella was a very strong person. She had her views and opinions about events and the people she met, but she seldom expressed them."

Ella did have two people that she could confide in and look to for support – Zula's parents Jadwiga and Paweł. She spent as much time with them in their apartment in Saska Kępa as she could and formed an especially close bond with 'Grandfather' Paweł who – unlike Zula and Artur – had the time to listen to her troubles and talk her through her fears. Her saviours were busier than ever working for the Home Army and saving lives but the one thing they knew was that saving her father would truly help the teenage girl they had come to think of as one of their own. Moshe had to be persuaded to leave the ghetto. Of that they were certain.

With his wife and son dead, and rumours that the ghetto was soon to be liquidated, in the spring of 1943, Moshe Złotnik finally agreed to Artur's offer to help get him out. He was grieving and alone. There was little business left and nothing more he could do to help his fellow Jews. An uprising was being planned in the ghetto and he knew that the German retaliation would be complete annihilation. It was time to be with his daughter.

Cleverly, and to distract her from her own grief, Artur and Zula enlisted Ella to help them prepare a suitable hiding place for her father. The small apartment they decided upon belonged to a wealthy landowner and former business acquaintance of Moshe's from the Mława region. Moshe used to buy grain from him and Artur also knew him through the bank so they had a double reason to trust him. The tenement building the landowner possessed on Pańska Street in Warsaw, a few blocks from where Ella and the family lived, had been partially destroyed, but the owner still lived in one part with tenants in another part and agreed that Artur and Ella could renovate a vacant one-bedroom apartment in the ruined section for Moshe. It would be a safe property to wait in for a while before looking for a more permanent place.

"Once we knew Father was coming, we prepared everything and my father paid for it, although we rented it officially in my name," Ella said. "The superintendent of the building knew me because I used to go and help set it up. He assumed I was the only tenant."

When everything was ready, Jowita explained that Artur took charge. "My father took him out of the ghetto through the sewers. It appears that someone else was there with them who led the entire escape, as my father had no clue about the Warsaw sewer system; he must have asked someone from the Home Army to help who knew how to walk underground in order to exit onto a correct street, and not for example onto a square in front of a police station, as happened to one of our acquaintances."

Warsaw's capacious municipal sewer system, designed by an English engineer at the end of the 19th century, had been used throughout the war for the frequent transportation of people, food, information and arms. Hundreds hid down there amid the sewage and the rats to avoid arrest, and escape to the Aryan side through the sewers became common. The Polish resistance known as 'sewer rats' used the network to reach key locations where they would lift manhole covers and launch surprise attacks on German patrols from behind. Because of this, the German soldiers developed something known as 'sewer paranoia' and frequently threw down grenades, killing or maiming those hiding below. They also blew up whole sections, blocked them off, flooded them with makeshift dams, or filled them with poisonous gas.

They lowered listening devices to hear voices or movement, so that everyone using the tunnels had to move about in complete silence in the stinking darkness, their hands on the shoulders of the person in front or on the walls to stop them from slipping over. The slow progress meant that those below were often trapped down there for hours as they carefully negotiated a complex network of tunnels filled with noxious gases. To even venture into the sewers took enormous courage and hundreds died in the dark – their bodies left for the vermin.

It was years later that Ella found out that her friend Ala Biberkraut had also escaped through the sewers around that time with her family, her boyfriend Jerzy Felenbok, his parents Jacob and Sabine and Jerzy's younger brother Paweł. In an account given by Jerzy after the war, he described how they carried only backpacks and were guided at night to a manhole cover near the wall by an Aryan smuggler named Juscek. They clambered down a ladder and, bent double under the low ceiling, followed the experienced guide through the labyrinth of stinking sewage-filled tunnels. Ala's father Benjamin was so weak that he had to be pushed through the tunnels in a wheelbarrow. They eventually emerged on the Aryan side and were hurried to a temporary safe house until they could be found somewhere more permanent. The group of friends and neighbours that followed them drowned in the sewers when the SS deliberately opened the sluice to flood the tunnels and flush out any escapees.

Artur was taking a huge risk in trying to save his friend and take him back to the Aryan side. He and Zula even promised to return to the sewers later to free Moshe's business partner in the ghetto, plus his wife and child, even though the Ghetto Uprising had started and the Germans were fighting back with heavy weapons and flamethrowers. Ella said, "My mother was gone already and when the ghetto was burning my father left through the sewers. Many people did it. And he knew exactly where he was going – to the apartment that was prepared for him, owned by a so-called friend."

Ella's reunion with her father after their momentous year apart took place in the privacy of his new hiding place. They had much to talk about and to grieve over together. Ella asked what happened to her mother and Moshe told her another story entirely, claiming that Celina had volunteered to go to the *Umschlagplatz* on a transport out of the ghetto because she was 'unable to bear any more nightmarish suffering'. She had no inkling that this might not be true. Once the talking and the crying was over, it was up to Ella to keep her father alive by visiting him at least twice a week with the basic foodstuffs he needed to survive, plus a dish of soup or some other meal to heat up. He couldn't risk leaving the apartment, so his days were long and lonely. Ella recalled, "I did not stay there. I would just come in the morning and do the shopping and prepare some food and stay with Father and then go out to take care of things."

Jowita said, "Ella entered the most peaceful period of time for her, if you can call it that at any time during a war – she went to school and she visited her father." She didn't go to the country with the girls that summer so that she could stay home and look after her father. Ms Nitecka, who had long ago stopped asking questions as she figured out who she was and became fond of her, prepared all the food she took to Moshe. The old cook also helped Ella do his laundry and wash and mend his careworn clothes, the same ones he'd been wearing since before the war. Aside from providing physical and emotional sustenance, Ella was able to bring her father the latest news, which was especially important for those in hiding, starved of information from the outside world. The Pieńkiewicz family gleaned most of their information from BBC transmissions listened to on an illegal radio and the news appeared to be getting better. After the Battle of Stalingrad the front was drawing ever closer, although the Poles had every reason to be suspicious of Russian involvement after their treatment by the Red Army in 1939. The only news Moshe would otherwise have heard would have been from the Germans who blasted Nazi propaganda several times a day from speakers placed in the streets that were known as the 'street barkers'.

News from the ghetto was of especially concern to Moshe, as the street barkers said nothing about the ongoing Ghetto Uprising, one of the largest single revolts of the war by Jews. It is thought that Moshe may have been involved in the planning of this historic campaign. By April 1943, the ghetto was full of rumours of that last great deportation being planned. In spite of this, the remaining Jews continued to prepare for their last Passover, with a few even able to prepare some food or obtain a little wine. On April 18, on the eve of Passover, news came that German and Ukrainian soldiers were poised beyond the walls and the ghetto would be liquidated imminently. Men, women and children mostly fled to the airless bunkers that had been prepared, stocked and fortified for them, praying and expecting the worse. The resistance fighters, meanwhile, made their own preparations.

That night, the Germans and Ukrainians entered the ghetto and began their last *Aktion*. Almost immediately, the Jewish underground – realising that they were on the brink of annihilation – resisted efforts by SS-*Gruppenführer* Jürgen Stroop and his men to crush them and deport even more families. It was a battle to the death for them, a chance to restore the honour of the Jews and shame the inaction of the Allies. One of the survivors said afterwards that, as they knew they were all likely to be killed anyway they decided to 'pick the time and place of our deaths'. Teddy Liebowitz, a friend of Wladek and Ala Biberkraut, smuggled a message out to them that said,

There will be a fight for every stone and window and, of course, it may be our end. In any case, you should know that I didn't go like a sheep!... A son's kiss for your mother. A brotherly kiss for your sister! To our quick meeting. Your Teddy.

A brave handful of rebels carrying handmade grenades, Molotov cocktails and other weapons managed to seize control of the ghetto, executing several soldiers along with their Nazi collaborators. The Germans were shocked by the level of resistance and retreated to gather more weapons, men and tanks. After three days of intense fighting, when Jürgen Stroop realised that the deportations would have to be abandoned, he instead ordered that the ghetto be destroyed with machine guns, by bombardment and then, later, burned down street by street and block by block. Thousands died in the ensuing firestorm, many of them suffocated by the heat and smoke, or burned alive as buildings collapsed in on themselves. In the confusion, many tried to escape via the sewers and flee to the Aryan side. Some made it with the help of the Polish underground, but most didn't.

One survivor said later, "I decided to leave and was met by an unimaginable sight. The cellar, through which our shelter was reached, lay in ruins, the electricity and water cut off. Through the holes in the walls one saw a sea of flames engulfing the nearby... building from top to bottom. Bilious smoke blocked out the sky... The courtyard was covered in shards of glass, pieces of brick, of tin, of charred wood, damaged piping and other debris. I was no stranger to destruction... but this surpassed anything I had ever seen."

Others reported that sparks from burning buildings were blown by a strong wind onto properties not yet alight, setting fire to everything. "People don't have time to flee the houses and perish inside in a tragic manner." Another reported, "People with bundles run from house to house, from street to street, there is no rescue, no one knows where to take shelter... The ghetto walls are completely surrounded; no one can enter or leave. The clothes are burning on people's bodies. Screams of pain and crying... Everything is in flames."

The Home Army, realising what was happening, fired on German positions and sentries at the ghetto gates in the hope of assisting the rebels, but their attempts to blow up a section of the wall failed. The surviving leaders of the Uprising were forced to flee through the sewers, tunnels and by whatever means they could. The remaining fighters and civilians cowered in the sewers and their cellars. Many of the rebels swallowed cyanide capsules as the Germans closed in, flooding the bunkers, or dropping smoke bombs to force them out. The Uprising officially ended on May 16, almost a month after it began, with the deaths of 13,000 Jews. The rest, amounting to approximately 50,000 men, women and children, were deported to Treblinka or Majdenek concentration camps. The ghetto's historic buildings and streets that formed some of the oldest districts of Warsaw were turned into what witnesses described as 'a sea of rubble'.

Gruppenführer Stroop cried '*Heil Hitler!*' when he pushed the button on the detonator that destroyed the Great Synagogue of Warsaw, the largest in the world with a capacity for 2,000 people. All that was left of one of the grandest buildings ever constructed in Poland was a cloakroom tag. Its eradication marked the symbolic end to the destruction of the Warsaw ghetto. Stroop declared afterwards, "What a marvellous sight that was... The will of Adolf Hitler and Heinrich Himmler had been done." He reported back to his Führer in Berlin that, "The Jewish district of Warsaw has ceased to exist."

Had Moshe Złotnik remained in the ghetto it is unlikely that he would have survived the Uprising. Although he'd been spared that fate, along with just a handful of other Jews, he was still in grave danger hiding on the Aryan side and the isolation was stifling. It was even worse for thousands of others, including the Biberkraut family who'd also managed to escape through the sewers. The entire family had to hide in the cold dark cellar of a ruined building for the next 15 months, never seeing daylight and living in constant fear of being denounced or abandoned by those they relied on for food and water. When Ala's father Benjamin died in the cellar, they had no choice but to bury his body in the earth beneath their feet.

Starved of conversation and wholly dependent on Ella for news, Moshe was grateful to the owner of the building and his son, a lawyer who lived in the same block, who started visiting him in the evenings to play cards. Those nights in his little bolt hole must have reminded him of the joyous bridge parties he and his wife had so enjoyed at the Pieńkiewicz home back in Mława. Moshe also had secret meetings with his former ghetto business partner, the man Artur had helped to escape along with his family and whom Zula had placed in a safe house. Ella said, "He met with his partner to finish up whatever business they had together and to split what was left, as there was no possibility of continuing their trade. It was a primal thing; they divided it equally. Whatever was left my father felt it wasn't safe to have with him in his apartment." Moshe suggested that Ella knock on the door of the man who owned the building and ask if he would secrete it somewhere for him.

"I went and spoke with him and he assured me there was a place to hide it. That afternoon Daddy gave me a package. I don't even know what was in it, but I told him it would be kept in a safe place. I went down to the owner's apartment and he showed me an old stove standing in the centre of the room that was only connected in the wintertime. He said, 'Open it,' so I did and it was full of ashes. He said, 'Put the package in there and cover it with ashes.' So I covered it up and I went up to Daddy and I said goodnight and went back to Zula's."

The following morning Ella went shopping for her father as usual and then walked to the apartment to deliver his food. "I looked in and the door was ajar. The whole place was a shambles.

Everything had been turned upside down. The mattress was all cut up where someone had been searching for things, and on the table was a notification for me to report for a hearing at Gestapo headquarters. I ran out and rushed very fast down the stairs and on the way down the superintendent barred my way and said, 'Stop right there! I cannot let you go.' I asked what happened and he took out a piece of paper and informed me that the Gestapo had been in the apartment. 'They knew you were hiding a Jew. They told me to stop you and take you to them. I'm supposed to stop you.'

"I told him, 'Impossible!' and started to argue. At that moment the owner of the building came out onto the balcony and saw us, and he started talking back and forth with the superintendent. He said, 'Listen, let her go.' The man let me go then and I ran away, but I didn't go home. I had learned from Zula that I should never go back home after any trouble because somebody could follow me, so I walked and walked and at a certain point I went to a public telephone on the street and I called Zula and told her exactly what happened."

Zula was, she said, 'terribly alarmed'. She told Ella to stay where she was and she arrived soon after and took the trembling teenager straight to the apartment of her parents Jadwiga and Paweł, with whom Ella was already very close. "She said you cannot come home. You have to change your name. We will have to start from scratch."

Jowita said, "Ella knew my grandparents very well; sometimes she stayed with them and they liked each other very much. Together they decided that she would remain with them, but this time she couldn't go out at all until one of my parents came with information that she could return. If they did not come, this would mean she must wait a little longer. As a last resort, if they were also arrested during Ella's absence, one of their colleagues who knew her would come to tell her where her new hiding place will be." Safe in the arms of her surrogate grandparents, Ella spent the next three weeks there, recovering from the shock and learning to cope with the growing dread that – in spite of all their efforts to save him and keep him safe – something terrible had happened to her father.

Knowing that the Gestapo could return at any time, Zula risked a great deal to go back to Moshe's apartment building and confront the owner. She demanded the package of money Ella had told her about, but he told her, "Get out! This is not your business. I don't have anything of his."

Ella said, "That is when it was obvious that once he looked inside the package and saw how much money it contained, he decided to get rid of my father. Some big friend he was. That's why he told the superintendent to let me go because he didn't want to make a big issue out of it; he just wanted his hand on the money. One hand was helping me while his other was killing my father. He paid for that after the war. The AK went to his house and killed him. The first thing Zula did was report him and order that he be killed."

Jowita remembered this also. "Father submitted the case of Mr Złotnik and the owner for review to the underground special Civil Court, which through trusted sources quickly determined circumstances of the detection. Mr Złotnik's former friend first got out of him all his money and valuables, then denounced him to the Gestapo. When the case of Mr Złotnik's arrest became known amongst their common acquaintances, the owner questioned about the circumstances claimed that he, himself, was being blackmailed by someone and this is why he had to take the money from Mr Złotnik.

"He said that when it ended the blackmailer threatened to denounce them both. In order to save his own life he was forced to go to the Gestapo first and report 'finding' Mr Złotnik, who apparently had just come to his apartment asking for help. He assured his acquaintances that he did not know the blackmailer, and this is why he cannot indicate him. The Civil Court did not believe those explanations and Moshe Złotnik's landlord was sentenced for collaboration with the Germans and blackmailing the Jews, with the penalty of death. This is how my mother relayed it to me, and one of her Home Army colleagues confirmed it in the 1970s."

Ella never truly discovered what happened to her father, and there are no records on file. Artur contacted his colleagues in the Home Army to ask them to find out but they came up with nothing. Purely by chance Ella heard later from a mutual friend who was taken to the Gestapo headquarters that day suspected of being a Jew that she had seen Moshe in a larger group of suspected Jews. "They were led from one room to outside. She knew it was my father and my father knew it was her and he stood next to her. She didn't even look at him. He just said, 'I am worried about...' And that was it, because the whole group was killed right there outside, so I know for sure that he was there."

Moshe David Złotnik, successful grain merchant, enthusiastic bridge player, devoted husband and father and a survivor of the Warsaw ghetto, was concerned about his daughter Ella to the very final moments of his life. The Nazis gunned him down in a bloodstained courtyard four years after they had robbed him and his family of his home and his happiness by invading their country. He was 42 years old.

Ella's grief at losing her father was overwhelming. They had only just been reunited and had developed a new bond as she brought him his food and clothing every day. They were the sole members of their immediate family to have survived, so each was all the other had. To have had him back and then lost him so cruelly not long afterwards was too much for a teenage girl to cope with.

For Jowita, Ella's sudden disappearance from their home came as a shock. "I returned from classes and found the house overcome by fear. Nobody said anything, but I sensed the fear. Ella was not there. In response to my questions about where she had gone, Mother told me that she went to the country to visit friends and would be back in a few days. Because no one worried about her, even Ms Nitecka did not ask questions, we stopped asking. After about three weeks, Ella returned and told us that she was visiting a friend and then our grandparents in Saska Kępa. And that was all.

Even when Mother informed us that Ella's last name was no longer Zabłocka, but Zakrzewska, we were not surprised – lots of people had different names. The nicest of the 'uncles' or my parents' colleagues who visited us very often was called Janusz Piechocki, then Paprocki, and finally something else. We only had to remember that we did not know his last name."

Many years later, Jowita asked Ella how she dealt with her father's death. After a long thought, she responded that it was quite different from the death of her brother and mother – deeper and even more difficult to bear. She said the presence of my grandfather and conversations with him helped her tremendously. "They didn't talk at all about Ella's father, or his death – these were conversations about religion, belief, philosophy and their views on death. It was clear to me that Grandfather had such conversations with Ella at the time she needed them the most. He must have felt that she did not want to confide about what had happened, this would have been too painful.

"She was in shock having lost her father, the last person from her closest family. She wanted to believe in something and Grandfather would have intentionally familiarised her with different religions and philosophical theories, moving her from the burning issues towards distant theories in order to give her peace and time to think. I was not surprised. I was only surprised that Ella got so easily attached to Grandpa. I was always a bit afraid of him. She was shocked when I said that and asked me, 'How come you were afraid? Your grandpa was goodness itself!' She knew him from another side. She thought he was the most even-balanced, wise and good man she had ever met in her life. She fell in love with both of my grandparents."

Jowita's grandmother, the redoubtable Jadwiga who had already lived through so much including the Russian Revolution, kept Ella occupied by instructing her to help her feed the birds in the garden, who used to tap on the kitchen window to demand more seed. Ella also read many different books, mostly on the history of Polish literature. While Paweł erected a small bomb shelter in the garden and played Bach's Brandenburg Concerto very loudly, Ella would sit with the old lady and look through her Russian family albums. By the end of her stay she was better versed on the family history than Jowita or Kalina ever were.

"I do not know whether she cried in the evenings, as she did after the loss of her brother and whether anybody consoled her," Jowita added. "I think that our grandparents belonged to the generation that was disconcerted rather than touched by shows of emotion, and although they would have been gentle and affectionate, they would not have sat with her without being asked to. Rather, they would try to busy her with something and listen if she wanted to talk. Ella herself was different by then anyway after more than two years of living in Warsaw during a war and in a double conspiracy. It made her – as my mother said – more 'salted' – and her strength and congeniality allowed her to make a faster return to everyday life, at least on the surface."

Ella only returned when Zula and Artur were certain that nobody appeared to be looking for her or had staked out their building. The duplicitous landlord, who knew of the family's involvement but was still awaiting his sentence from the Home Army at that time, didn't dare report them to the Gestapo. Ella received her new identity papers as Elżbieta Zakrzewska and returned to her old routine as best she could, throwing herself into her studies in preparation for her matriculation. Her grief at her father's death weighed heavy on her young heart and she was often found weeping privately. She said, "I didn't know if my father had made it. And I was hysterical. Zula would take me into the little room – her office – and she would close the door while I cried."

Zula did all she could to lift Ella's spirits but she knew she had to work through these feelings on her own. The teenager dared not go out so much for fear of being apprehended by someone who recognised her from her father's hiding place and because of the ongoing risk of being taken to service the soldiers. Instead, she stayed inside and lost herself in her books. One day, when she was heard crying in the apartment again, everyone ran to see if she was alright, Zula at the fore. All were relieved to discover that she was only weeping over the storyline of a tragic Gothic novel she was required to read for her final grade. It was called *The Wages of Sin* by Polish author Stefan Żeromski and told of a young girl tricked into bed by a married man who ends up killing her own child and attempting to murder her lover before she sinks into prostitution and is ultimately killed. Jowita said, "Mama was glad that she could release her tears through fiction when the truth was too hard to bear."

The people of Warsaw never stopped their struggle against their oppressors and Artur continued to work in the Golden Beehive, by then as deputy director in charge of the theatre's finances. Zula continued to carry out the orders of Colonel Suszczyński to the north and the east, using her excellent German and the fake documents which identified her as Zofia Pauser, a Wehrmacht officer's widow, a role she rehearsed carefully and dressed down for. Hoping to cheer Ella up and to make her feel useful again, Zula enlisted her help to make her look like a dowdy German *Frau*. Ella said later, "You should've seen how much this amused Auntie!" The teenager was already privy to so much about Zula's work that it didn't seem worth keeping her out of the loop, although Zula was careful never to share any names and addresses with her or anything incriminating, just in case she was ever interrogated.

Another thing Zula came up with, undoubtedly to cheer Ella, was to send her to stay overnight with her cousin Janka, a woman who made her living during the war baking cookies. The favourite aunt of Jowita and Kalina for this reason alone, Janka had a contact in the *Volksdeutsche*, someone who was part German and was therefore entitled to better food stamps and access to items ordinary Poles could never get hold of. In this way, she procured sugar, butter, flour and chocolate with which to make her cookies for the cafés that served the Germans. Best of all, there were always pots of leftover chocolate which she allowed visiting children to scrape out. Ella was sent to Janka's immediately after the Easter holidays because Artur and Zula had invited guests who would have to stay overnight because of the curfew. Jowita was extremely jealous.

"Cakes during the war were made from a dark, meagre flour, German margarine with a little bit of lard, saccharine instead of sugar, and imitation chocolate made by boiling beans and mashing them with molasses of sugar beets. They were nothing like the delicious and wonderful cookies Auntie Janka made. Ella, while staying in her safekeeping, helped her with her work and was able to scrape off the sweet substance. Kindly, she bought a bun home for each of us."

And so life went on. Artur and Zula's work continued to be vital to the efforts of the Polish resistance, the Jews in the ghetto, and the Allied intelligence, but change was in the air. By early 1944, Italy had surrendered, the Germans and Italians had given up North Africa, and the Siege of Leningrad was over. These momentous events cemented the idea that the Germans might lose the war, raising spirits and hopes. After five terrible years the innocent families caught in the crucible of history dared to think that this could finally be the end. For the first time since the outbreak of the war, the decorations of the 'Lord's Tombs' on Good Friday and Holy Saturday had expressed not pain and sadness but hope for a resurrection. Could the Polish people allow themselves to believe that their suffering would soon be over?

6

CAPTURE

It was 4am on April 18, 1944, when the family was abruptly woken by loud banging on the locked metal gates to the front and rear of their apartment building. They heard German voices shouting, followed by even more insistent banging.

"It was at that time of night when you are most deeply asleep and far away in your dreams," said Jowita. "The sound of that banging stayed with me forever. For years afterwards, if I heard something in the night I would wake up and lie so stiffly that I couldn't move or be moved. That night, within seconds of our rude awakening, everyone jumped out of bed until the occupants of the entire building were up and on their feet."

The family was given only a few minutes to hide their valuables and brace themselves for invasion while the building's caretaker Mr Wróbel (a member of the Home Army), deliberately took his time in finding the right keys to unlock the huge lock on the heavy wrought iron gates. "My parents were clearly very shocked and had no inkling that this was going to happen, or they would have moved Ella. They got up immediately and lit candles. We had no electricity that night, as it was not our turn. First, they checked to make sure anything illegal was hidden. Father threw his gun into the ash pan of the cold stove that sat in a dark corner and Mother kicked a briefcase – in which she kept the jewellery she'd been buying for the previous six months – under the huge *szafa* or wardrobe in the dining room. They hid our valuables too and then they started to get dressed. With all this to do, and the shouts of the Germans getting closer and closer, there was no time for them to run down the stairs to the basement and escape through the cellars.

"Mother told Ella to wear her dressing gown and put on some underwear but not a dress, so that it wouldn't look as if she was getting ready to flee. We waited for the caretaker to open the gate wondering which apartment the Germans would go to. The soldiers were still banging and shouting. He took so long that when the soldiers finally tore in through the gate, they attacked him with their rifle butts. At that point, there was absolute silence on all six floors."

In the courtyard the Germans separated into several groups and efficiently blocked every entrance to the building. After a while the family heard the clatter of their jackboots on their stairwell followed by loud banging on the doors of their apartment from the front and from the kitchen. It was them they had come for. Ella recalled, "I was back living with Zula and preparing for my final exams when the Gestapo came. They were looking for Zula and her husband." As the noise grew louder, the petrified Jowita and Kalina huddled against Pamaja's legs in their nightclothes, all of them too afraid to move or even speak.

Ella said when Artur opened the front door, the intruders burst in and began rifling through the whole apartment. "They started with me and seeing that I had a lot of books around me, they asked, 'What kind of books are they?' throwing them around, deciding that this or that was illegal." Jowita recalled that the five men, including two Gestapo officers in uniform, seemed very well informed about the layout of their home. They quickly scattered into the various rooms, shining flashlights into the faces of the occupants, who stood shivering in their nightclothes. They showed no interest in Pamaja, Ms Nitecka, Miss Linka, or the two little girls, closing the double doors to the parlour after they had checked who they were. Instead, they continued to turn the place upside down and to focus only on Zula, Artur and Ella.

Jowita still shivers at the memory. "We were so very afraid because, although we lived with the fear that we could be killed at any moment, German soldiers had never come to our apartment before. And of course we didn't even know then how dangerous it was – with a Jewish girl, the Jewish owner of the flat, and two members of the resistance in our midst. In the dining room the Gestapo gathered only my parents and Ella. We couldn't see anything because they had closed our door, but I heard shouting and my father falling down. I had no idea what they did to him but learned later that Mama had said something to calm Ella and had taken her hand and a German had shoved her away at which point my father had jumped in to defend her and was beaten to the floor."

Straining to listen and frozen in terror, Jowita said she and Kalina and Pamaja stood by their beds as if they were statues. "I didn't understand anything the soldiers said in their fast-barking screams, but I could hear only calm responses from my mother. Unfortunately, she had hidden almost everything from them but forgot to check her nightstand where, the previous evening, she'd carelessly thrown one of her false IDs – the German one with her photograph but the name of Zofia Pauser, a Wehrmacht officer's widow. If they hadn't found that then everything might have been different."

The Gestapo informed Zula, Artur and Ella that all three would accompany them to their headquarters and ordered them to get dressed. At Zula's insistence, they allowed Ella to change quickly in the bathroom, while she and Artur were allowed into their bedroom one at a time, with the door half open so that the Gestapo could ensure that they wouldn't try to escape. The previous evening Zula and Artur had been to the Name Day party of a friend so she pulled on the evening dress she'd been wearing the night before and Artur put on his suit. Before being taken away, Zula demanded a few moments to say goodbye to her children. She wore a fixed smile as she drew her young daughters into her arms – a moment Jowita will never forget.

"They didn't want Daddy or Ella to kiss us goodbye. When the door opened, I couldn't see them in the room beyond, just the two officers. Under the supervision of a soldier standing in the doorway Mama came in very elegantly dressed and kissed us goodbye. I was weeping and told her, "What will I do? I will never see you again!" She was a very strong person but she almost collapsed then. She said something and smiled and then she whispered to Pamaja to take care of us. Pamaja told her, "Of course I will. I promise," and she then marked the sign of the cross on Mama's forehead. Then they took the three of them away."

Jowita doesn't recall if she cried out that night, but admits it is likely. Later – in prison – her mother wrote a heartbreaking poem about that it, in which she said:

> ... I hear in my ears banging at the door!!!...
> Here they come! Press your lips
> Until they bleed! "Open the door."
> No! Nobody is in the resistance here
> "These papers on the desk?" They are mine!
> Children? Yes. Two.
> "Get dressed!"
> The sound of revolvers cocked
> And the door slammed shut and a cry
> A child's cry – I can still hear it in my ears.

When the door slammed shut behind the departing Gestapo and soldiers, Jowita said, "Throughout the whole apartment building there was a truly deathly silence then. They didn't take anyone else from any other apartment, just from ours. In the courtyard we could hear the steady tramp of boots and, in contrast to their military rhythm, the sound of Mother's little steps in her high heels. It was a sound that haunted me for years. Then it was silent again.

"After a long while Pamaja knelt by the bed and prayed, then she got dressed. I was still weeping and Kalina was bewildered and scared. Pamaja went to the kitchen and we followed, terrified of losing sight of her. There we found Ms Nitecka and Miss Linka kneeling by the table and also praying. Pamaja asked the cook to start a fire under the stove to make something hot for us all to drink." After a steadying drink of apple peel tea Pamaja warned the girls and the two spinsters that the drama of the night wasn't yet over. If the Germans behaved according to their usual pattern, they would return to conduct a more thorough search. She was right. Within two hours, they came. This time, though, it was just two Gestapo officers who arrived without their guards, in order to rob whatever they could find. "It was still before the end of the curfew at 6am, and each one had a large briefcase. They went around the apartment selecting all those things they had noted on their previous visit, packing everything they liked into their briefcases: a silver tray with a full silver tea set, a tiny 18th-century porcelain and enamel clock (one of Mother's souvenirs from her time in France), Father's gold pocket watch. They took a little table and chair in the lobby and a beautiful silver filigree dish with a matching cake slice – Russian heirlooms that were passed from my grandmother to my mother. When Ella came to live with us, she brought very little, but one thing she did have from her mother Mrs Celina was a little set of silver cutlery for one person – a knife, a fork and a spoon as well as a little fruit knife and a teaspoon – with a pretty apple decoration on the handle. It must have been given to her because it was precious, or because it invoked certain happy memories. It came in a little leather box, but that was taken too.

"The Gestapo stole everything of value for themselves and not because they were ordered to. They spoke quietly and did not argue – they looked especially for gold and money. They tipped out Father's desk and asked Pamaja where my parents kept their money but she pretended not to understand German, even though she spoke it very well, and started crying loudly. The Germans emptied the closets, throwing everything out, and finally they left as quietly as they came. They never found the jewellery or the gun."

All her life, Ella could hardly bear to recall the events of that night. She told Jowita later, "I had one thought. I was only afraid that they would separate us. I knew that all three of us would not go to jail together, but I prayed that I would stay with Auntie, and not be all alone in this world." She did not remember anything else at that point, nor did she want to remember or talk more about it, although she did later.

As the three prisoners and their captors rode together in the back of a Gestapo truck through the darkened streets of Warsaw, they passed through the heavily guarded security cordon around the Jewish ghetto. Artur, 48, knew for sure then where they were going and that he would imminently be separated from his companions with no chance to say goodbye. Their final farewells consisted only of loving glances and a brief squeeze of his 35-year-old wife's hand as he was climbing out of the truck. Their destination was the notorious Pawiak Prison in the heart of the Jewish ghetto. Built chiefly on the site of Ulica Pawia, or Peacock Street, it was the largest and cruellest Gestapo prison in the whole of Poland. Since the German invasion in 1939, more than 100,000 prisoners had passed through its high walls and forbidding wrought-iron gates. Of those, 60,000 were transferred to prisons, concentration camps, or for slave labour.

An estimated 37,000 were murdered during interrogations or executions, and 20 prisoners died every day at the hands of the Gestapo as well as brutal German and Ukrainian guards. The Home Army tried their best to stop this mass slaughter but the prison with its high walls, watch towers and barbed wire was unassailable. There were a few successful ambushes of prisoners en route and five SS officers and two female prison guards were shot dead in the street. In February 1944, just two months before Zula and Ella arrived, Hans Burkl, the sadistic deputy commandant of the prison, was also assassinated but still the killings went on.

On arrival, Artur was led into the main four-storey building that housed men of every class and race, including Jews, the clergy, the intelligentsia, political prisoners, and those suspected of being in the resistance. Zula and Ella were herded into the three-storey female section of the prison to the left, which housed women and children, including some 25 babies born in the prison. This wing was named 'Serbia' after its time as a military hospital during the 19th-century Serbian war. Originally designed to house approximately 700 inmates in total, at its peak capacity under Nazi-rule Pawiak incarcerated almost 3,000 men, women and children, which meant there were as many as ten prisoners to cells intended for two. Zula and Ella were pushed into the dank, dark cell number 15, a small room that already accommodated four other women, some of whom had been sentenced to death.

The prison built between 1829-35 was primitive, cold and dirty and the prisoners had to sleep on the floor or on wooden planks covered with thin straw mattresses that were crawling with bedbugs, fleas and lice. The sanitary arrangements consisted of one metal can and there was very little food or water. There were frequent epidemics of typhus and scurvy and the prisoners suffered from boils, the breakdown of their skin and malnutrition. The single small window in Zula and Ella's cell provided not a breath of air to combat the smell of fear and unwashed bodies. Despite the vile conditions, the other women treated Zula and Ella kindly and immediately helped them find a space in which to sit and await their fate. As it was clear that neither of the new arrivals had ever been in jail before, the other women filled them in on what life was like in the so-called 'Peacock Jail'.

The chattiest of all were two were sisters from Silesia in their early thirties named Katarzynka, known as 'Inka,' and Angelika, known as 'Gela' Guzy. Described by one of the prisoner-doctors who worked at Pawiak as 'extremely brave and courageous', the sisters were fluent in German as well as their native Polish, which they spoke beautifully. The region of Silesia had been under intense pressure for years from first the Prussians and then Hitler to become *Urdeutsche* or historically German. Its people were encouraged to speak only German, to the extent that whenever they spoke their native Slavic it was with a marked German accent. When Zula asked the sisters why they spoke such excellent Polish they told her, "Our father loved Poland and made us learn the language correctly. Whenever we spoke German, he'd chastise us and say, angrily, 'Do not use these *Schwab* expressions for I cannot stand them!'" (Schwab being a Germanic tribe from Bavaria and used at the time as an insult.)

Under occupation, both sisters had to give up their studies and work at the regional rail headquarters in the busy junction town of Katowice, in the office that directed train movements. Having been raised as staunch Polish patriots they were happy to assist the resistance against the Nazis. Their inside knowledge had been indispensable to the Home Army, as they had delivered secret reports on the movements of German soldiers and munitions to the Eastern front, as well as transports of Jews and others to Auschwitz. They were too good, though, and the Germans realised that information was being leaked. They were arrested in Warsaw in May 1943 and then interrogated and tortured but refused to divulge any information. Inka was especially harshly treated and was placed in solitary confinement at Pawiak for a long time, while her sister Gela found work in the laundry. Designated as 'Germans' by the Nazis, they were eventually convicted of treason and sentenced to death by beheading in Berlin, but there was confusion as to the manner of their death as their official sentence stated that they would be hanged in Pawiak. Hence, they waited in limbo to learn if they would be beheaded or hanged by their necks until dead in this prison or at a concentration camp, where many prisoners were sent for execution.

Despite this terrifying prospect, the sisters were courageous, amusing and friendly, and did everything they could to welcome Zula and Ella. They quickly explained that all of their cellmates had been arrested on suspicion of belonging to or collaborating with the Home Army. Nevertheless, they assured them that they were lucky to have been placed in cell 15, as it was designated for prisoner-functionaries only. This meant that they'd be allowed to work, which, in turn, should mean that they received a little more food and a few privileges such as extra barley in their soup or cigarettes for those like Zula who smoked.

Jowita said, "She met very good souls in that cell who quickly recognise that she was a Jew in hiding and firstly ensured that she was ready for interrogation, although nothing could really prepare them. Both she and my mother had never been in such a situation and it was necessary to prepare them for the German interrogation methods at Gestapo headquarters." The women assured Ella that the Germans wouldn't guess she was Jewish but began to question her about religion just in case. Ironically, they decided that she had been too well prepared even for a so-called Christian.

"She knew the principles too well and when one of them asked, 'How many buttons are there on the priest's cassock?' Ella without hesitation replied, 'Thirty-three!' She was the only person in the cell who knew that information, as regular Catholics wouldn't concern themselves with such details. Nor did they teach that kind of thing at school. The whole cell discussed it and decided that only a person who either dealt with priest's clothing on a regular basis, or someone who'd been taught far too well would know this. They ordered her to forget this information immediately and, if asked, reply, 'I have never counted.' They also advised her to pretend to appear stupid in general, a young girl busy with only household chores and her studies. They all came to like her very much: she was the youngest, very sweet and helpful. They treated her as a 'daughter of the regiment.'"

Every day, the prisoners stopped talking or even breathing whenever they heard the guards approaching, their keys rattling as they prowled the jail looking for their next victim – another anti-Nazi to beat, torture or murder. Executions without trial were carried out daily and some of the guards were known for their bestiality. Twice a day, the Guzy sisters informed them, a truck known as the 'Hood', or the 'Black Maria' would arrive at the prison morning and night to collect 50 or so hapless inmates and ferry them to and from Gestapo HQ. After a few days, the guards came for Zula and Ella too, driving them terrified from the sanctuary of their cell and into a black vehicle known by the prisoners as a *buda* or kennel, because its occupants were treated like dogs. As its siren wailed, they would have cowered together in the back under the black tarpaulin, expecting the worst.

Their destination was the most feared building in all of Poland,

25, Szucha Avenue, the Gestapo headquarters and interrogation centre south of the city in an area exclusively occupied by Germans. Originally built in the late 1920s as a centre for religious beliefs, the imposing art deco building with its fluted marble columns at the entrance was requisitioned by the Nazis in 1939. Anyone who survived being interrogated and tortured there was either sent back to Pawiak to recover for the next interrogation or was sent to the *Umschlagplatz* next to the railway station in Stawki Street. There they would be packed into open freight wagons or cattle cars and sent to the death camps, following in the footsteps of some 250,000 Jews deported to Treblinka from the Warsaw ghetto. Hundreds more were gunned down in the Kampinos forest on the outskirts of Warsaw, where their bodies were added to vast mass graves.

In the building's basement were ten narrow cells known as *Strassenbahn* or 'trams', into which any new suspects or so-called 'undesirables' were forced to sit upright on hard wooden benches facing the wall as they awaited their fate. They were often left in total darkness and could hear the screams of those being tortured during 'examinations' upstairs or nearby. The Nazis used iron-tipped whips, truncheons, electrical equipment, medical instruments, ropes, cigarettes, dogs, manacles and other instruments of pain to torment their victims. They were often hung by their feet and had water poured into their mouths and noses. Toenails were torn out and bones broken. They might be smothered with defective gas masks, burned with hot irons, or endured forced enemas that burst open their stomachs. Those who refused to speak would often have their families tortured in front of them. The prisoners awaiting their turn were forbidden to sleep and were given nothing to eat or drink for days at a time. The bullet-pocked walls bore testimony to what had happened to the ones who disobeyed the rules, and many did not survive their time in these cells.

Zula and Ella were taken down to the cells together but then Zula was hurried away, leaving terrified Ella alone with the sounds of suffering all around her. As Zula was taken past the *Strassenbahn* cells to be interrogated, she thought she glimpsed Artur briefly from behind. A man who looked just like her husband sat alongside other male prisoners under armed guard, with his back to the corridor. Tragically, she didn't dare call out his name or even confirm that it was him in case he was shot for even turning to look at her. Then she was pushed upstairs.

Downstairs, Ella waited and waited, listening for every footstep. Later accounts suggest that Zula's interrogation could have taken as long as 18 hours. After what must have felt like an eternity, the guards came for Ella too. Two men ordered her to go with them and they walked her down the long jail corridor. It was all she could do to put one leg in front of the other. Halfway along the corridor Ella looked up to see Zula being carried back to the cell on a stretcher. She would never have recognised her but for her distinctive evening gown. Her beloved 'Auntie' was lying on her stomach, but when she lifted her head at the sound of approaching footsteps, all Ella could see was a swollen, bloody face, its features deformed through violence. The face she thought she knew twisted into a ghastly contortion as Zula recognised Ella and passed her by. She was too weak even to raise a hand.

A few minutes later Ella sat down in front of the interrogators whom she realised must have been the same men who had beaten Zula so horribly. In that small room with bloodstains on the floor and the fresh smell of violence, Ella's quivering was no act. She told Jowita later that she 'played a deathly scared teenager', which is exactly what she was. Jowita added, "The interrogators didn't bother her for too long – after all, she was not the one they wanted – they came for my mother, and Ella was arrested only according to their rule of taking all adults (over the age of 16) from the homes of suspects for checking. They asked her a few questions about her relations and the activities of the people she lived with and then ordered her to return to prison. The greatest ordeal for her was the sight of my beaten-up mother."

Ella concurred. "With me they were rather gentle. They asked me questions and I answered the truth. I knew nothing. I did not know any names and they knew that I wasn't lying. They didn't even have my name on their list. They were trying to find out what they could from me and I told them that I did not know anybody. For some reason they believed me." The family later learned that the reason the Gestapo had been tipped off about the family in the first place was because a new recruit to the Home Army in Zula's division had been arrested randomly in the street and taken for interrogation. Under torture he began to tell them everything he could to stop the pain. This 'boy soldier' knew very little and, although he would have recognised Zula by sight, she didn't believe he knew her real name.

Beaten and abused, however, he gave up a whole list of people, all of whom were subsequently arrested. He told the Gestapo of a woman named Pieńkiewiczova who was personally unknown to him but worked for an officer in the headquarters and who could therefore identify all the senior officers and their addresses, including the important one known as 'the Divorcee'. That is why Zula's home was targeted and she was arrested, along with Artur and Ella, because they happened to be home that night. As they were her closest family, the Gestapo decided that there was a chance that they could know something too.

The terrified teenager returned to Pawiak unharmed to find Zula had been cleaned up by the women in their cell and was lying in a corner, semi-conscious. "There wasn't a place on her body that wasn't black and blue. They couldn't even move her in the cell." She was so beaten up that she couldn't speak for two days and when she did, she told them what had happened during her interrogation.

"Two Gestapo men began by asking her about her false *Kennkarte* and her family, and then they started to read off a list names or nicknames of wanted Home Army men, asking which she knew," Jowita said. "For the longest time she responded, 'I do not know,' until finally she heard the name Szreniawa and answered, 'I know!' The officers almost jumped out of their chairs and demanded, 'Who is it?' Zula looked at them and smiled. 'The main character of a book I wrote in my youth,' she answered jokingly.

"One of the Gestapo men suddenly hit her with his fist with full force. Something crunched and she spat out some blood and four broken teeth. 'Pick them up!' ordered the officer and when she bent down, he pulled her up by her hair, pulling out a clump. They then tied her legs and hands and pushed her onto the table where they began to beat her with either a stick or the leg of the broken chair that was lying next to her. Every now and then they repeated their questions and continued beating, attempting to find out the name and address of 'the Divorcee', not realising it was her own nickname. That was when she realised that someone must have informed on her from within her own unit. She didn't speak any more, so they carried on beating her. When she passed out for the second time, they called the prison guards and ordered her to be sent back to Pawiak 'temporarily'. She was being carried away when she saw Ella."

Ella later asked Zula why she gave her such a ghastly grimace when they met in the corridor. Zula answered, "It was a smile! I wanted to smile to give you courage." Later she admitted that she was as terrified of torture as everyone else but that nobody knows their resistance to pain or how they'll react. "For her everything was decided on the first blow," Jowita added. "She claimed that as she leaned over to pick up her teeth and the German pulled her up by her hair, she felt as if she were slowly turning to stone. 'I thought, 'Oh, so this is how it is? Well, then. Now you can kill me.' The rest I felt as if through a fog, even the pain itself.' She did not remember how long it lasted, but she recalled that one of the Gestapo officers cursed how hard his job was. Beaten all over from the neck to the tailbone, with broken ribs, a sore head, and internal bleeding, she was sick in the cell for more than two weeks."

Ella nursed Zula attentively in the cell with the help of the other women and was also assisted by the prison doctor Dr Anna Olga Czuperska, whose underground pseudonym was *Dr Podkowa*. The doctor was 36 years old when she and her husband Henryk were arrested in November 1940 for being members of the Union of Armed Struggle (ZWZ). Henryk died two years later in Auschwitz. After being interrogated and tortured, Dr Czuperska remained a prisoner-doctor at the infirmary in Serbia for the next four years and became head of the women's prison intelligence unit. She and her colleagues facilitated contact between inmates so that they could synchronise their stories to the Gestapo, and they saved lives by insisting that certain prisoners were not well enough for further questioning. Dr Czuperska also used Latin to convey sensitive information.

The Nazis only allowed medical personnel to work within Pawiak in order to keep the prisoners alive so that they could continue to interrogate and torture them. They also feared contagious diseases such as typhus and put the doctors in charge of sanitation and hygiene. Through the work of the Association for the Care of Prisoners, known as *Patronat*, volunteers looked after nearly all aspects of the prisoners' lives, giving them extra rations, and providing medical and pastoral care. The Germans had no idea that it was these same doctors and nurses who did the most to alleviate the suffering of the prisoners and to assist in their ongoing resistance activities. Anyone who was brought to them after being tortured would be met with kindness, compassion and the words, "Don't worry, child, you are amongst your people now. Did they get something out of you? Who should we warn? Give us the addresses."

Time and again Dr Czuperska and her courageous colleagues braved death to save beaten, mutilated women from being sent to the camps or returned to Gestapo headquarters for more brutality. In 1943, she found herself in a group of prisoners condemned to be shot but survived thanks to the intervention of a Gestapo doctor. After the war, she said, "There were times when we simply couldn't imagine how much a human being could endure, and how it was possible to survive such horrible, inhuman interrogations and extreme tortures."

The handful of doctors, prisoners and friendly guards at the centre of the conspiracy risked their lives daily to carry secret messages. They were transmitted either verbally, learned off by heart, or written on tiny notes known in prison slang as *gryps* (kites). These would be folded very small and smuggled in and out of the prison in anything from pens to razors, the shafts of heavy keys, inside buttons or hidden in the sleeves of clothing.

In *Pawiak: Martyrdom and Heroism*, Regina Domańska writes:

The systematic information flow about the situation in Pawiak relied on the efficient functioning of the intricate grid, consisting of courageous and sacrificial prisoners, ready to go wherever circumstances demanded. Prisoners with enough ideas to distract a prison guard from the person from or to whom you should pass the secret message. Personal contact between prisoners was extremely difficult. Hence prisoners wrote secret messages on the scraps of tissue paper with tiny (pencil) leads. Delivery to another prisoner or participation in handing them out involved mortal danger. Nevertheless, people taking part in this conspiracy did not hesitate... Every day through their hands passed hundreds of secret letters, which had been delivered even to prisoners placed in strict isolation. In the face of their own destruction, they took care of the beaten, fed the hungry, and contacted prisoners of a common case to agree on their testimony, which often determined their lives.

One doctor, Halina Borkowska-Holtrop, said of their work, "Generally our function in the resistance movement was to distribute secret messages. Our ordinary hospital coats always had their sleeves rolled up and, in those rolls, we placed secret messages. Of course, there was always a problem how to set those messages free and deliver them to families. Dr Wacek came to the hospital from outside and I gave him the secret messages."

Dr Irena Kononowicz, codename *Nono*, also helped the inmates by secretly delivering food to the female prisoners, carrying secret messages, or putting people in touch with those arrested for the same reason. Her optimism and hopefulness had a much-needed calming effect on the female prisoners, in a place where few expected to survive. One thing is clear: without the help of these brave souls, the death toll at Pawiak would have been much higher and might well have included Zula and Ella.

With the help of Ella, the other women in the cell and the medical staff, Zula gradually recovered her health but still lived with the constant threat of further interrogation or the discovery of Ella's true identity.

Both women had been given the status of *NN Häftlinge* or 'anonymous prisoners', which meant that they had no rights to letters, packages or any contact with friends or family, as other prisoners were. Fortunately, because of Zula's status within the Home Army and thanks to the doctors and to sympathetic Polish guards who only worked at Pawiak under duress, they received a few illegal packages and even some shoes for Zula, who had only high heels. Zula also managed to secure a job alongside Gela Guzy in the prison laundry, another place where she was able to pass messages to the outside world, with the help of Inka who worked in the prison post office.

Ella said, "Right away Zula got in contact with somebody who worked there too. Two or three of the guards and helpers worked for the underground so she quickly made connections. She sent *gryps* or little letters that went back and forth to her friends and family on the outside to let them know she was alive. They were written in tiny handwriting on thin cigarette papers that were then rolled up and slotted inside cigarettes or put into the bread. Most of them were instructions about her children or were personal letters to them. She prayed they were OK and she was worried about her parents."

The morning after the Gestapo took away Artur, Zula and Ella, Pamaja had taken Jowita and Kalina to their grandparents in Saska Kępa. She was determined to tell them what had happened in person. They all stayed there for a while and Jowita remembered her grandmother cooking her a hearty breakfast while Pamaja and her grandfather talked. It was decided that they should go back to their apartment for the time being. The following day, Jowita was sent off to her secret school lessons as usual, feeling numb and dazed. It was what Zula and Artur would have wanted, Pamaja insisted. Three weeks later, though, it was agreed with their grandparents that the children should leave Warsaw for fear of an insurrection, so they went with Pamaja to the village of Chylice, south of Warsaw, where – through the Home Army – the family had been renting a two-room house for them to spend the summers. There, they received encouraging messages from their mother in Pawiak. Jowita said, "In the country we were told that my parents and Ella were in good health but that they would stay in prison for a while and that the war would end very soon. We knew nothing of the *gryps* or anything else about their activities in case we accidentally told someone. I was worried, of course, and I didn't quite know what to think. It was as if we were living two lives – one that was life and quite normal, and one in which death was always near."

In her tiny notes to her father Paweł from Pawiak, Zula also begged for news of her husband.

I am afraid for Artur in case they want to interrogate him in the presence of the children. I am also afraid that your name might be used. I am afraid for him and the consequences. You must do as you think right. Don't be anxious about me. I am stronger than you think. I kiss you all. Zula.

It was later that the family learned that on May 24, 1944, one month after his arrest, Artur was released from the Gestapo headquarters on Szucha Avenue as a *Schutzhaftling*, a vague term meaning protective custody, given the prisoner number 035911 and recorded as 'A, Polish' destined for *Arbeiter* or work. This meant that he could not have broken down under what could have been weeks of torture or interrogation, or he would have been executed. Instead he was loaded into a cattle wagon with others to be sent to an unknown fate. On a piece of paper he hastily scrawled his name and details plus the name and address of Zula's father Paweł, asking anyone who found it to let him know that he was being sent north to a camp in Stutthof, 20 miles east of what is now Gdansk. He then threw the scrap of paper out of the little window. Incredibly, some kind person found it and took it to Grandpa Kaliniecki, so that they would at least know where he'd been sent. Jowita has it to this day.

Stutthof was the first Nazi concentration camp set up beyond German borders in 1939, and one of the last to be liberated in May 1945. An estimated 85,000 prisoners of the 110,000 deported to its boggy woodland near the northern coast perished there. Most died of disease, starvation, or exhaustion from forced labour, but a month after Artur's arrival the camp's gas chamber was opened and its extermination programme was further supplemented by mobile gas wagons.

The news of Artur's whereabouts was passed back to Zula because in one of her next *gryps*, written to a girlfriend at the theatre, she wrote:

God bless you for a piece of good news about Artur. Please make sure that they constantly send him a lot of parcels. If you have difficulty with cash, I can forfeit my packages. In the first parcel send him typhus vaccine. Here, there is also typhus in the men's ward. Write him from me verbatim: I am indeed well, I am happy that he reached his place healthy, and I love him and will be praying for him all my life.' Write, even a small word to me and save Ella! ... I kiss everyone in the theatre... Give me back my sandals because I have nothing to wear here. Z.

The family did write to Artur and, incredibly, he wrote back (this time from a subcamp of Stutthof called Pölitz), sending overly cheerful postcards to his two young daughters. He told them that Daddy missed them and would be home soon. Jowita said, "We could write to my father and I still have postcards from him in Pölitz, a camp where the V1 and V2 bombs were made, using slave labour. He wrote back in the compulsory German via my grandparents – one written by him and one by someone else and asked for food."

Jowita was convinced she would see her beloved Daddy again and clung to the memory of the last time he had kissed her goodnight. "The night before he was taken and just before they went out to their party, Daddy came in to kiss us goodnight. I remember that he sat on my bed and we had a very serious chat. He said, 'You know I love you very much, my dear,' and then he spoke about being a parent and that was it – within a few hours there were men at the gate and I never thought I would see him again. When I received his postcards and Mama's letters, though, I believed that I would see them both, especially my father who I adored."

7

FINAL DAYS

Although Zula had survived her interrogation and hadn't cracked, she couldn't forget that she had only been sent back to Pawiak 'temporarily' and was terrified that she would not be as strong under further torture.

Jowita said, "Ella confirmed this. She said that Mother was afraid of nothing except that she and Artur be interrogated and tortured in front of the children, which they often did in Pawiak." Zula knew too much about the Home Army, including their responsibilities and the names of the members of her unit. "Through the female doctors who had contact with the Home Army, she asked for some of the cyanide which was available for those on the most perilous missions. She received an answer that the command was trying to send her to a camp or to work in Germany and that the negotiations were underway regarding the bribe that needed to be paid." The message was that Zula was too important an officer to lose and had become a hostage who would fetch a handsome ransom for a corrupt Nazi, of which there were many as the war increasingly looked set to end in the Allies' favour.

Paying bribes to senior German officials and guards was a common practice throughout the war but was especially risky in a high-security prison such as Pawiak. Bribing them with cash or expensive gifts helped persuade them to look the other way or allow a prisoner extra privileges. In 1943, Irena Sendler, a Catholic social worker who is credited with rescuing 2,500 Jewish children from the Warsaw ghetto, was arrested and tortured by the Gestapo in Pawiak and at its Szucha headquarters. Her legs and feet were badly broken but still she refused to betray her network of helpers. Eventually, the organisation she worked for bribed a guard and she was freed, to resume her activities in hiding.

Like Irena Sendler, Zula's first thought then was not for herself, but for Ella, and she insisted that she wouldn't leave without her. She demanded that the young woman she'd grown to care for as her own was included in the negotiations. The theme of rescuing Ella became a recurring one, as Zula gave little thought to her own fate. In a note to her parents, she wrote:

Mummy and Daddy! God bless you for the card and the news; it is such a joy for us. For God's sake what is happening with Ella? If it cannot be done differently, let her go with me to the camp, but the case against her is nothing and she should just go home. I pray a lot. I am really healthy and working doesn't make me tired, only the thoughts about you, children, and Artur. God will bless you that you remember about him. I will survive and endure everything if they do not execute me, and you take care of yourselves, so we will still see each other. Let me know when the Holy Masses, which I have asked for, will happen... I kiss your hands. Z.

Her cigarette paper pleas repeatedly begged, *Save Ella!* pleading for the life of her young charge. This became her focus and her priority. Zula said later, "I knew I was going to be shot but I couldn't bear the same fate for Ella. Her mother had begged me from the ghetto to save her child. I promised her then that I would make every effort to do so." When the Home Army seemed less than inclined to save a teenage girl unaffiliated to their organisation, Zula argued that Ella knew enough of their activities, especially the smuggling and the underground activities at the Golden Beehive Theatre for the Gestapo to widen their arrests if she broke down. She further claimed that alone in prison the teenager could easily fall apart, especially under interrogation. The commanders at

Home Army headquarters accepted the validity of her arguments and Ella was finally included in the negotiations.

Jowita said, "Mother hoped that such negotiations would mean that the Germans, at least for now, would leave them in peace. She had already become a bidding commodity and she waited for the outcome." It was around this time, never knowing if the Gestapo might come back for her at any moment, that Zula secretly wrote a poem for Ella called *Night in Serbia:*

> At night, in a narrow sliver of the sky shine a few
>   cool, faraway stars.
> Don't say anything to me. I know. No need...
> 'Hundreds of villages taken and a few cities...'
> Lying together, staring into darkness.
> Listening to the breathing of sleeping heads.
> Don't speak that someone weeps in despair. I know.
> Me... I am also without words.
> In the distance, the city is sleeping.
> Over the ruins a spotlight shines ghostly from a
>   tower.
> Don't speak, that sorrow falls with my tears
> We don't know tears. Not you, not me.
> The sound of rattling keys and someone's steps!
> He's getting near! Did he stop? No, he has passed.
> Today, only nine executions.
> Don't say, 'Not for us', because the time will come.
> When the pale dawn falls through the bars of the
>   window
> We will fall into the deepest sleep, without dreams.
> Shots will wake us! And then?...
> Don't speak. No need... I know without having to
>   hear the words.

The timing of the negotiations to free Zula and Ella was crucial. By May 1944, with the German army retreating from Russia, the officers of Hitler's war machine realised that they faced an uncertain future. Terrified of what the Russians would do to them if they won Warsaw, many started planning their escape, a journey for which they'd need all the money and valuables they could get their hands on. All were far more open to bribes than they would have been at the beginning of the war, although their demands were often eye-wateringly high.

The worst part for Ella and Zula was not knowing what was going to happen to them. They might not even die at the hands of the Gestapo – epidemics of infectious diseases were picking off the inmates of Pawiak at an alarming rate and still the interminable waiting went on. In an uncharacteristically negative note, Zula wrote to her family.

You do not realise how much I value each card. Even just a few words save me. For God's sake, send me the things from my list. For those prisoners who have some duties one can send packages more often – twice a month. Let Artur write me once and give me his address and I will write to him under someone else's name. Father, please don't undertake any legal proceeding or official requests to the German authorities. If you cannot release Ella from here then try to influence them that she is sent with me on the transport. Answer the questions! Send us cigarettes without filters because we can take more of them, and four boxes of matches... Send me cigarette papers. They are executing five to ten women every second to third day. Kisses for all. Z.

On May 16, 1944, Ella turned 20, an event that – were it not for war – would have been celebrated happily at home in Mława with her parents and younger brother Ishay. Instead, she was wasting away in a filthy cell with no idea if she'd be the sole member of her family to survive. Kindly, her fellow prisoners arranged a birthday surprise to cheer them up. Each of them was allowed packages from family and friends with a few little delicacies that were highly cherished. Yet the women saved up all their special treats and threw Ella a Name Day party. They even managed to procure a small basket of flowers and a white linen tablecloth from the German laundry of the kind that would have been used at officers' tables. As soon as the guards had completed their final evening round and all the cells had been inspected, their little party began.

All was going well until they suddenly heard footsteps and the door to their cell was thrown open. The prison commander stood in the doorway. There was no time to hide anything so they all sat rigid with fear. He walked in, took a good look around and said, "Yes, in such conditions I would also like to have a good time."

The gutsy prisoner Inka Guzy, in perfect German, retorted, "Oh no! You will serve your time in a completely different way."

The Gestapo officer stiffened, stood very still for a few agonising seconds, and then left with his entourage. The women regarded it as a small victory and Ella reminisced about this incident fondly for years.

Knowing there was nothing she could possibly give her as a gift, Zula wrote her surrogate daughter another, far lighter, poem about the moment she had freed her from the ghetto in Saxon Gardens, and recited it to her on her birthday:

> A vegetable garden slept in the August heat
> while in the distance the world silently fell,
> I looked into the pale, tired faces –
> I chose you as if I picked a flower.
> Pale, passive, you came with me,
> not even knowing why and where.
> That bright morning for you was dark,
> and everywhere strange and everywhere bad.
> As days and months passed,
> you grew into my heart through fear and tears...
> Surely now in no separation
> will I forget you or you me.
> I had once promised that I will save you,
> That I will guard you as my own
> God will forgive me that I don't defend you,
> I, who is like a shard, like a thing.
> Today is your holiday my little one –
> The only present that I will give you:
> Let my song sway you –
> I give you my heart – it's all that I have.

Their happy celebrations were spoiled within weeks, however, by the news that Zula had been tried for her crimes in her absence and was sentenced to death by hanging. Although the negotiations were still ongoing, until they were finalised to the satisfaction of all sides no one knew what the Gestapo might do or whether they would renege on their promises. Then the Guzy sisters were taken away, which led to tearful farewells in their tiny cell. Inka was sent to Stuttgart to clear debris and rubble from the Bosch factory that produced parts for the Luftwaffe and was bombed repeatedly by the Allies. Angelika's fate is unknown.

As the days turned into weeks and weeks into months, and without their cheerful, witty friends to keep their spirits up, the frustration and the fear of what might happen to Zula and to Ella began to gnaw away at Zula. Smoking whatever cigarettes she could get hold of, her letters became uncharacteristically bitter as she complained of epidemics of diarrhoea and typhus. In one, she wrote to her two daughters:

Jowita and Dolenko. My dears, I know that three months is a long time and your life goes on. I am not surprised that you are slowly forgetting about us. But please write a few words sometimes. It's the only thing left to us here... Please send us photographs. Please send the package I asked for twice. This will make easier the moment of waiting for death and you two will finally be free of thinking of us.

As June turned to July, Zula knew that she and Ella were still far from safe.

After months of delicate and dangerous negotiations, the Home Army finally found the corrupt Nazi they needed at Gestapo headquarters in order to get Zula and Ella out. The man whose greed was greater than his loyalty to Adolf Hitler was Hauptsturmführer Nadolny, a mid-level commander with a Polish surname and a rank equivalent to a captain.

Having agreed to consider a bribe, he demanded an astonishing 140,000 *młynarkis* or occupation złotys to convert Zula's death sentence to one of transportation to a concentration camp, and a further 80,000 *młynarkis* for sending Ella to work in Germany. The exchange rate at the time was between two and four *młynarkis* to a Reichsmark so his fee was around $50,000, the equivalent of $700,000 today. His final condition was that the money was to be exchanged into American dollars at the current rate and paid in gold coins, which would be easier for him to dispose of. The leadership of the Home Army debated whether or not to pay the bribe and how to raise the funds.

An officer visited Zula's parents Paweł and Jadwiga in Saska Kępa to keep them informed and see if they could help. Jowita said, "Someone came to see my grandparents to tell them what was happening. Ella was easier to liberate than my mother because she wasn't wanted by the Gestapo and her name hadn't appeared on any list. Her background in Lvov couldn't be corroborated because of the proximity of the Russian front, and they assumed she was just an innocent girl who happened to be in the same family. My mother was much more of a problem, as she was of great interest to the Gestapo, who were confident that they'd extract information from her under torture, so it was important to get her out."

In her *gryps* to her parents Zula told them of the jewellery hidden under the wardrobe in her apartment and also said that she had 40,000 Deutschmarks in the books, all of which could be used to help pay the bribe. The jewellery was found, but not the cash. Jowita said, "My grandfather didn't know if she meant it was money hidden in the books or maybe the value of the books so he came to the apartment and checked every single one. For two days he was there with Pamaja checking, but they couldn't find anything. In the jewellery he found, though, were some things he kept back for me – my gold medallions from my first Communion and a gold ring of my mother's with beautifully cut turquoise stones and a matching bracelet. There were some other beautiful things from my mother, and they were treasured belongings." As the delicate negotiations continued, and Pamaja and the children and their grandparents waited anxiously for news, Nadolny's conditions were finally accepted and the money was somehow found and paid. He converted Zula's death sentence to imprisonment and arranged for her to be sent to Ravensbrück concentration camp.

For Ella there was better news. In mid-July 1944, she finally received her papers releasing her from Pawiak. She was to be taken to the so-called *Dulag*, an *Arbeitsamt* or employment exchange on Skaryszewska Street in Warsaw, where those prisoners not to be executed or deported to concentration camps were checked and registered before being sent for forced labour in Germany. What the Nazis didn't know was that the Home Army had something else in mind for her. Dr Czuperska had contacted the Home Army doctors working at the Dulag and forewarned them that Ella was to be designated too unwell to work because of a kidney complaint. She asked them to alter her test results and analyses so that she could be freed. The blood and urine samples of someone with a genuine renal problem would be substituted for hers in case the German supervisors checked their findings.

Jowita explained, "The doctor instructed Ella before leaving Pawiak that at the time of her medical check-up she must complain about kidney pain, and then act according to her instructions. Once she was released, someone she knew would be waiting for her at the entrance to Poniatowski bridge on the right-hand side from the direction of Prague, and this person would take care of her."

Ella had hardly been parted from Zula during the previous three years and in prison the pair had become inseparable. Now, as Zula briefed her about where to go and what to do once she was free, Ella realised that she was going to walk out of Pawiak while her beloved 'Auntie' remained locked up, her fate uncertain. Once again, she would be on her own.

Even more worryingly, as the Russians moved closer from the east, it seemed possible that neither of them might get out in time. Ella said, "There was a time when the Russians were approaching already. The Germans started liquidating signs of their crimes including Pawiak. So they started going through all the cases of people that were supposed to be killed and those to be sent to work in Germany and they sent them all away."

Her parting from Zula on July 19, 1944, was emotional as they embraced and bade each other a tearful farewell. "Let's hope that we meet again someday," Zula said through her tears. As her daughter Jowita said, "Ella was as much a support to her as she had been to Ella. She couldn't have got through it without her." It was Ella that Zula had been able to focus on throughout which meant that from then on, she would have nothing to distract her from her own fate. As a parting gift, she handed Ella a flimsy piece of paper, the type used to carbon copy letters on a typewriter. On it were the words to *The Garden,* the poem she'd written for her, which she'd had secretly typed up by one of the Home Army members who worked in the prison office.

Zula reminded Ella that the theme of the poem was that she'd made a promise to her mother that she would keep her safe; a promise she now feared she hadn't kept. As she was no longer able to care for the young girl she'd seen blossom into womanhood, the poem was all she could give her as a talisman. Ella took it gratefully and vowed always to keep it with her. She kept that fragile scrap of paper almost until her dying day.

When the cell door opened and Ella's name was called, she went rigid with fear. In spite of all Zula's promises, she was convinced at first that she was going to be executed. Instead of being taken to her death, however, she was driven to the Dulag as promised. In the four-storey brick building where she spent the next two days undergoing a series of medical tests, she played her role well, doubled up in pain as she went through all the necessary examinations under the supervision of Home Army medics, one of whom remarked, "You look so sad." Constantly watched over by German doctors, she was anxious until the moment they finally agreed that she was incapable of physical work and should be released.

"She walked out of the door, down Zieleniecka Avenue, through Skaryszewski Park to Waszyngtona roundabout, revelling in the spring sunshine and the warm summer breeze blowing off the nearby Vistula – her first breath of fresh air since April. This was the only memory from the war to which she returned willingly and with a smile," said Jowita. On Poniatowski Bridge Captain Janusz Piechocki (also known as Paprocki) – a once frequent visitor to Zula's apartment – was waiting to meet her with what she called his 'pre-war' smile. He gave, she said, the appearance of a serene young man without a care in the world.

He took Ella to a flat at 11 Chałubińskiego Street, the home of Tadeusz Śliwczyński, the forger who worked as a clerk in the courthouse on Leszno Street and who'd provided many of the false documents the Home Army needed. His son Jerzy and daughter Lala also lived in their small apartment near the central station and Ella remained with the family for several weeks, trying to return to some sort of normality. Mrs Śliwczyński was especially kind to her and did all she could to make her feel welcome. Ella liked her very much and never forgot her kindness. After a while, though, she was given her own place to live in a village outside Warsaw for a while because there were too many other people hiding in the Śliwczyński flat. The family reportedly helped a doctor and his family, a pharmacist, and his family, and two other women. Ella returned to Warsaw once they had been found other safe houses to live.

Alone again, Ella was prevented from visiting Zula's parents Paweł and Jadwiga in Saska Kępa or Pamaja, Jowita and Kalina in Chylice, as that was considered too risky. It was a kind of torture for her to be kept away. As Jowita said, "It was discussed whether she should go to my grandparents, which she would have loved, but in the end the Home Army decided to send her where she had not been seen before and where there would be no rumours surrounding her. That must have been very hard on her – she had lost everyone then and was denied the comfort of being with the people she called Grandpa and Grandma."

Tadeusz's granddaughter Malgorzata Kozikowska said, "Ella lived in my grandparents' flat for some time. Although people who lived in the building knew about Ella's origins, they never betrayed her. I know she frequently went out for walks, to the cafés and that she accompanied my family to various social and family meetings... People, especially the young, tried to lead as normal life as it was possible at that time."

Normality wasn't something that Ella had known since the first day of September 1939, and – despite putting on a brave face with her hosts – she knew that she had no one, with both parents, her brother and grandparents all dead. Her fervent hope was that Zula and Artur would survive and she could one day be reunited with the brave family who had saved her life.

Two days before her departure to Ravensbrück in July 1944, Zula wrote a final heartfelt letter to her family pretending to be happy that she was being sent to a concentration camp.

My beloved parents, daughters, Mary (Pamaja) and Ella. Farewell and until we meet again when the time has come. Take care of the children and of each other and try to rescue Artur. Today is the 19th and so much joy... Pray for me and thank God for saving me. I am kissing your hands and feet. I am sending hugs and giving blessings to my beloved daughters. I beg Mary for protection and heart... God be with you, Z.

Her letter to her daughters was just as poignant.

Jowita and Dolenko. Some day when you will be adults someone who cares for you will give you this. It will be proof that your parents were killed while serving Poland. Take bravely on you this legacy of ideas and go through life proudly and honestly. Have respect for yourself and for everyone. See the humanity in every person. Respect your guardians because it is difficult to take care of other people's children. Remember that your father was a man without any flaw and very lonely in his life. Every year on July 20th go to the Holy Mass and pray for us. We already said farewell to you. God be with you because we both believed in Him deeply. I do not want to impose anything on you. I ask only for your forgiveness that we made you orphans so young. Be healthy, honest and happy. Love each other because you two only have each other in this world. Until the last breath of life I will pray for you and bless you. Your mother, Pawiak, 1944

Ravensbrück was more than 500 kilometres away in northern Germany and 90 kilometres north of Berlin. It was a camp exclusively for women, most of them Polish. The majority were political prisoners, and there were also 26,000 Jews. Of the 130,000 women who passed through its gates during the war only 15,000 survived until liberation. Towards the end of the camp's life, an estimated 80 women were dying every day from disease, starvation, or overwork. There were some 70 sub-camps, using forced labour for munitions and to feed the German war machine, and medical experiments were also carried out in this camp.

Zula was sent there in a sealed cattle wagon, the Nazis preferred method of transport, a journey that took several days without food or water. She arrived on July 22, 1944. Her prisoner number was 45749. All new arrivals had to wear a colour-coded triangle that identified them by category, and Polish women wore a red one with the letter 'P'. Zula was no exception and was assigned work in a Kommando working for the German Siemens company in a factory making radios for ships and planes and parts for VI rockets, while subsisting on starvation rations. Unbeknownst to her, Inka, and Angelika Guzy, with whom she had shared a cell, were also sent to Ravensbrück one week later, on August 1. The sisters managed to find work running a little shop; a place where prisoners could buy items to supplement their diets. Sadly, the camp was so large by then with an estimated 50,000 prisoners spread out over a vast site, many of whom were sent away for slave labour, that the three were never reunited and Zula always wondered what had happened to the kind young women who had helped make Pawiak more bearable for her. Jowita said, "She always said that the people of Silesia should know how brave and wonderful those *Urdeutsche* girls were."

Within weeks of arriving, Zula became seriously ill with scarlet fever. The friends she had made in the camp did all they could to help her and had someone steal anything from the camp hospital they could find that might help her but they only had aspirin. She'd wake in the night burning up with fever and suffocating in the overcrowded hut where everyone slept two to a bunk.

Desperate to cool down, she'd stagger to the bathroom and lie down on the cold floor alongside the bodies of those who'd died that day. She was so seriously ill that her friends feared she wouldn't survive, but then – somehow – she rallied, thanks to the help of a Jewish prisoner-doctor she later credited with saving her life.

Reassigned to work in the administrative office which was less demanding, she was typing something one day when her friends approached her with long faces. Jowita said, "Mama was very sensitive and she knew something had happened. 'What is it?' she asked, and they handed her a piece of paper. 'It's about you,' they told her." The paper was a typewritten order that Zula Pieńkiewicz was sentenced to 'death by hanging, after one year'. It had been authorised by Nadolny. This might possibly have been because he suspected that the war would be over in a year and the sentence would never be carried out, or because he wilfully chose to renege on the deal he had made with the Home Army. The vague wording meant that Zula had no idea from what date the year was to be marked – her arrest in April, her so-called 'trial' in June, or her arrival at the camp? If it was the first then it would mean that, unless she died of something else first then, with usual German efficiency, she would finish her days at the end of a hangman's noose on April 18, 1945, having endured nine months struggling for survival in a concentration camp.

Looking up at her friends, she smiled and said, "Oh, don't worry. I was expecting something like this." Her friends in the camp later described her as, 'fearless', which is what enabled her fast thinking in finding ways out of difficult situations. As such she was often the one who took command.

As in Pawiak Prison, Zula found an outlet for her inner feelings through poetry, writing several that featured in a book of camp poems that survived the war. She spoke of the 'monotony of grey days' in 'gloomy grey buildings' and the 'boredom of everyday fear'. She described sleeping on rotten straw and wooden planks, the endless *Appells* where 30,000 women had to stand in silence for countless hours as the rain soaked through 'these miserable clothes'. She wrote of the few hours of darkness where she lay 'like a chased and wounded animal', and the flames from the crematory chimney that formed the words, 'My beloved daughter. Keep well!'

One poem, called *At Night*, summoned the memory of being rudely woken in the middle of the night and taken from her home and her children:

I lie with my hands behind my head
And stare directly into the darkness...... for a long,
    long time...
I lie for an hour, for two, until I see on a dark wall
As if the wall were a bloody screen. These images
That keep on coming back
The images cut through my head like a sharp knife
They crush my head like heavy stones
...and again there is fresh blood in a dry wound
...I hear in my ears banging at the door!!!...
Here they come! Press your lips
Until they bleed! "Open the door."
No! Nobody is in the resistance here
"These papers on the desk?" They are mine!
Children? Yes. Two.
"Get dressed!" The sound of revolvers cocked
And the door slammed shut and a cry
A child's cry – I can still hear it in my ears
The screen is dark. As dark as it was there
In the basement, in a small cell
And then awfully bright
When they took me out...

She also wrote about her interrogation, which had no break or
moment of relief:

Enough! Enough! Enough!
I will not tell you! No, I will not tell you!
A broken bone cracked
Some torn hairs stayed in their hand
And suddenly: the voice lowers "Take her back to the
    cell!"
Some red light on the screen
A bleeding man on the screen

Nobody is able to help me. To comfort me. To give
   me some advice
I must face it and get through it all alone
Through some sticky fear of death
Fury and despair
Helplessness and rebellion
'Halt Mund!!!'
Yet I hear every day the same
A distant child's voice saying 'Mama!'

Within days, Zula had more bad news to digest. As she had feared, the long-expected insurrection to liberate Warsaw from the Germans as the Russian Red Army approached from the east began on August 1, 1944. Led by the Home Army, it was supposed to last a few days only and was timed to coincide with the mass German retreat from the Soviet front. The plan was that just as the Russians arrived in the city, the resistance fighters would strike from the centre and the two-pronged attack would push the Germans out.

Zula would have been desperately worried about her parents and Ella in Warsaw but grateful at least that her children were out of harm's way in Chylice. What she didn't know was that Ella would be evacuated from her safe haven as the fighting intensified and that her father Paweł had summoned Jowita, Kalina and Pamaja back to the city on July 31, believing that they'd all be safer together. They arrived at Zula and Artur's apartment just a few hours before the shooting began.

The largest single military resistance against the Nazis throughout the Second World War got off to a promising start but was then fought bitterly for 63 days with little or no outside support. The tragedy of the Warsaw Uprising, as it became known, was that the Red Army reached the outskirts of the city and then stopped on the east bank of the River Vistula, from where they could see and hear the shooting. Stalin declared that the Polish resistance fighters comprised 'a handful of criminals' and were 'inspired by enemies of the Soviet Union'. On his orders, the Russians did nothing and the

British felt their hands were tied without their permission. Churchill's appeal to President Roosevelt that they defy the Russians and intervene fell on deaf ears. This political stalemate gave the Germans time to regroup and call in reinforcements to crush the insurrection. An estimated 150,000 civilians and some 6,000 soldiers were killed and a million people displaced.

Once it was all over, from September 1944 to January 1945, the Germans used flamethrowers and dynamite to destroy what was left of the once-beautiful city on the orders of SS chief Heinrich Himmler, in accordance with Hitler's express wishes. He said: "The city must completely disappear from the surface of the earth and serve only as a transport station for the Wehrmacht. No stone can remain standing. Every building must be razed to its foundation."

On the eve of the Uprising, Paweł and Jadwiga had planned to meet their grandchildren and Pamaja at Artur and Zula's apartment but when they set out they found that the bridges were already blocked and they couldn't get through. Devastated, they went back to Saska Kępa and waited to see if their little family would come. "From the roof of their house they could see houses on fire in our district and they didn't know what had happened to us. From there for 63 days they observed the fight to the death of the left bank of Warsaw during the Uprising. Grandfather was beside himself with worry," Jowita said. "Later, the Russians came and threw them out when they took over the right bank of the Vistula. The house where my grandparents lived, located close to the river, was well suited as an observation point."

The couple, who were in their late sixties, had already lost so much in their lives, were pushed along with other residents to the district of Grochów in Praga Południe. Jowita didn't discover until after the war that they spent the next ten months in the basement of a building on the eastern fringes of Warsaw, half-starved and freezing in what turned out to be the bitterest winter in European history for more than a decade. The effects of that winter were devastating for their long-term health.

In the city centre, Ella and those who were helping her were also under fire. Their home was near the central station, which was bombed in the third week of the Uprising, so they were also forced to leave for a time. Ella spent those 63 days moving from safe house to safe house, further away from the fighting each time. At one point she was taken to the village of Świder, a place on the river not far from Warsaw. Tadeusz's granddaughter said, "Before the war it was a popular holiday destination and I think Ella and the people who accompanied her went there to spend time in fresh air. It was as dangerous a place as any other at that time in Poland."

Pamaja and the children were also in grave danger. They spent the first two weeks of the Uprising hiding in the basement, listening to the shelling and the guns, until on August 14 the Germans came and told them, 'Everybody out! This building is to be liquidated.' Jowita said, "The Germans then herded us into the courtyard along with several hundred other people. They locked the gate after us and made us stand up against a wall. Some people wept, expecting to be shot. The house was set on fire and the streets around us were burning. Then the Germans gushed a beautiful liquid down the steps into the cellars. I remember watching it, mesmerised, like the curious elephant in Rudyard Kipling's story, seeing the liquid shining and iridescent. It was beautiful. When they lit it, the liquid burned immediately and so brightly. The Germans didn't shoot us after all. Instead, some ladies came with some food and water for the children while the men were looking for somewhere to hide inside because of the smoke."

Forced to flee as the Germans crushed the Uprising, they ran into the street, with only what we could carry, and hid in a ruined house. "That was the first time I met death because we had to get over a fence and I was too small to jump and there was the body of a Polish man staring up at the sky and I had to step on him to get across. I will never forget it. The next day the Germans ordered us out and said that house was to be liquidated too. Daylight didn't happen the following morning. It was as dark as night with black billowing clouds and just a small circle of the sun, like a Holy Communion wafer. It was shockingly hot."

Unable to tell if it was day or night, Pamaja and the children were then sent to Piłsudksi near the Tomb of the Unknown Soldier.

Everyone was supposed to line up to be shot but then somehow the orders changed and they ordered us to go into the Saxon Garden and lie down on the grass. I remember lying in the park and looking up and seeing all the tracer fire and the lights and the flames. We were so very hot and thirsty that, in the night, we children went to the duck pond and drank directly from the rancid water, lapping at it like dogs. The whole town was on fire and we were sent for sanctuary to the All Saints Church on Grzybowski Square, which was packed with refugees from the fighting, including one woman who cried all night as she was in labour. I didn't know it was that church until after the war because we spent almost all day getting to it through the ruins and it felt very far away."

The following morning they were marched to the railway station, where they saw something very unusual – soldiers dressed in black and speaking Russian. "They were Ukrainians who were collaborating with the Germans. The people were so very afraid of them. They said they were crueller still and would shoot on order without even looking. My sister Kalina, then eight years old, was such a beautiful thing that Pamaja tried to hide her from them. One of them spotted her and commented on 'the lovely little Polish lady', but there was something about the way they said it that frightened us." The three of them were packed into a cattle wagon with dozens of others, all fighting for air and water. They were transported to Pruskòw, a small town east of Warsaw and then after three days to work on a farm in Holzkirch in the Lower Silesia region of Germany, near the town of Lauban (now Lubań). The whole process from their first eviction had taken two weeks, but it felt like months to the two small children and their guardian.

"Pamaja saved us many times over. She loved us and I liked her, but we didn't really get to know each other until we were in Germany. I was 11 years old and Kalina was eight and always very good. I was a bad child and she would often scold me so that I was afraid of her. In Germany, though, I helped her. She had a weak heart and almost fainted sometimes and when someone stole the wooden planks they had brought us so that we wouldn't be sleeping in the bare ground, I stole someone else's to make her more comfortable."

The Russians eventually entered Warsaw on January 17, declaring that they had liberated Warsaw, when they had only liberated mountains of snow-covered rubble. By then the majority of the buildings had been destroyed, including the 700-year-old Old Town. There was no housing, electricity, water or sewers and what roads still existed were heavily mined. Almost every inhabitant lost all that they possessed, including the Pieńkiewicz family. Some 200,000 civilians had been killed in total along with an estimated 9,000 Germans. The rest were scattered to the winds. The city was uninhabitable by then and Ella, who had been moved around the city earlier on, had already been evacuated to a small village to labour on farms surrounding the town of Łowicz, where she remained until the end of the war. Jowita said, "She was sent to agricultural work. She had no idea where we or my grandparents were."

It is impossible to know how much Zula and Artur would have been told about the devastating events in Warsaw but, if they heard anything, they must have been terrified for their family, and especially for their little ones. All communication lines with the city were destroyed and there was no way of reaching anyone who could tell them of their whereabouts.

In Ravensbrück, Zula was still awaiting her death sentence to be carried out while fighting for her life. Not to be defeated, once she was restored to health, she decided to stage a cabaret in her barracks by way of distraction.

Despite the fact that some 50,000 of the 132,000 women and children who passed through Ravensbrück died, including 2,200 who were gassed, the camp had better facilities than most. The all-female inmates were able to create different cultural distractions and set up classes for the children. With typical verve, Zula worked out that she would still have time before her execution to organise her show for her fellow prisoners and, drawing on her experiences at the Golden Beehive, she came up with a cheerful script and set about raising morale, not least her own.

Jowita said, "She collected artists from amongst the prisoners – a famous Polish dancer from before the war; Russian and Ukrainian singers; a Czech painter who, from blankets and rags brought from 'Canada' (the stores of belongings taken from new arrivals), managed to conjure a stage design; and some other talented volunteers who were taught by the artists as much as possible. Together they put on their show in the large bathroom of her barrack late on the evening of April 1, 1945. It was a holiday revue and had to be repeated the next day, as it was so popular. A planned third show never took place, however, as the *aufzjerki* (overseers), started to suspect something and guarded the prisoners more closely after the roll call."

April 18, 1945, came and went and, to her surprise, Zula wasn't hanged. In her mind, that meant that her execution would take place in either one month or in three. She had no doubt that it would happen as the Germans were rigorously efficient. Fate intervened with the news of the Red Army's rapid approach. Hearing the guns, the SS commanders decided to remove or destroy as much evidence of their war crimes as they could. In the final desperate weeks of the war, more than 6,000 women were murdered in the camp's gas chamber and in mobile trucks, others were shot or starved and the rest sent on death marches north. Of those who remained, 500 of the women too weak to march were saved at the eleventh hour by the Swedish Red Cross on April 24, 1945. It was one week before the Russians finally liberated the camp and found fewer than 3,500 prisoners alive.

The extraordinary evacuation organised by the Swedes happened thanks to the efforts of the man who became known as 'the Swedish Schindler' – Count Folke Bernadotte, a diplomat and nobleman who was Vice-President of the Swedish Red Cross and a grandson of the last king of Norway and Sweden. Having successfully organised prisoner exchanges of Allied airmen in 1943 and 1944 that brought home 11,000 prisoners from Germany via

Sweden, the Count then negotiated personally with Heinrich Himmler for the release of more than 30,000 prisoners from Nazi concentration camps in 1945. Originally they were only Scandinavian but eventually included several thousand others of Polish, French, British, Czech, American and other nationalities, including many Jews.

The mission took two months between April and May 1945 and involved more than 300 Red Cross personnel criss-crossing Germany and Poland in a snaking convoy of vehicles that included ambulances, military trucks, cars, motorcycles and even fish vans. A total of 6,428 women and 413 men were saved, although 79 of both sexes died on the journey before they reached Sweden. The Count's mission became known as the 'White Bus Rescue', named after the distinctive white buses with the Red Cross emblem painted on their roofs so that they wouldn't be mistaken for military targets. The convoy was often shot at as it evacuated back across the devastated war-zone with its tank traps and barricades under heavy Allied bombing. And after the Germans painted their buses identically in order to facilitate their escape from the Allies, the danger for the genuine buses was massively increased. Once in Denmark, Danish and Swedish civilians then helped evacuate the prisoners to Malmö and beyond to recover their strength in Swedish hospitals. They were put on ferries or transported in a 'Dunkirk-style' flotilla of boats.

Those Ravensbrück prisoners fortunate enough to be selected for the final and most daring of the Swedish mercy missions at the only camp the Red Cross could now feasibly reach, had their coloured triangles unceremoniously torn from their uniforms by the guards and were ordered to line up. Zula Pieńkiewicz was amongst them. As they waited, Russian Katyusha rockets illuminated the sky and the artillery pounded the earth close by. Many of the prisoners hid when their names were called out, as they believed the rescue to be yet another Nazi trick to take them to the gas chambers. After years in captivity they had come to believe that a transport anywhere meant only death. For those who believed the Swedish men in grey uniforms with red crosses on their arms were genuine, their tortuous journey north-west to the Danish border had to be made along almost impassable roads and their convoy was machine-gunned in an Allied air attack, killing 17. It took three days but they eventually reached the Danish border via the cities of Schwerin, Lübeck, Kiel and Flensburg.

When the final ferry from Copenhagen arrived at the quay in Malmö on July 10, 1945, and the emaciated prisoners began to disembark in their ragged, filthy clothes, several waiting nurses fainted at the sight of them. A few of the prisoners, seeing the white-coated doctors and imagining them to be SS, became hysterical. Others were said to be 'the happiest human beings' witnesses had ever seen. They had cheated death and, once recovered, would be able to return to their loved ones and find out who amongst them was still alive. Top of Zula's list was the whereabouts and well-being of Artur and her children, and of her surrogate daughter, a teenage girl named Ella Złotnik.

8

A NEW BEGINNING

The Second World War finally came to an end in Europe with the German surrender on Wednesday, May 8, 1945. Adolf Hitler had committed suicide one week earlier. For millions of people across the continent, there was little joy to be had in their freedom. So many lives had been lost, so many people were still unaccounted for, and huge swathes of land and property had been decimated.

Ella was in the Polish countryside when she heard of the Armistice. By then, she had lost her mother, father, brother and both sets of grandparents, as well as many aunts, uncles and cousins. She was one of an estimated 5,000 Jewish children to have survived in occupied Poland, many in hiding, some in monasteries, and a few saved by individuals such as Artur and Zula. All that she had known in her happy childhood in Mława was gone and her country was in ruins. The fate of those who had saved her life was unknown and she had no one left in the world but her parents' siblings in Palestine who she barely remembered as they had all emigrated before the war.

Dazed, and in only the clothes she stood up in, Ella made her way back to a broken Warsaw to look for the Pieńkiewicz family. The sight that greeted her was shocking. The city was hardly recognisable and, with streets obliterated, it was difficult to find one's way through the towering piles of rubble. Trams stood burned out where their tracks had once been, and ragged people carefully picked their way through uneven corridors of glass, stone and concrete. Those buildings that had survived stood blackened, hollow and empty-eyed, and a thick grey layer of brick dust and ash that had settled gave everything a ghostly appearance. The apartment block where Ella, Artur and Zula had been arrested was no more. All that remained were six feet of foundation walls upon which desperate people had stuck notices seeking information about their loved ones.

"Pinned to every brick or rock still standing was all this graffiti, flapping in the breeze – little notes on which people had written their names and the fact that they'd returned to Warsaw and where to find them," she said. These poignant notes said things like: *Mummy, I came back from Germany. Where are you?* or *Stanislav, the baby and I are alive! Find us at the railway station* or *Grandpa, I will wait for news at the church in Kobyłka. Send word there.* With no other means of communication, the crowds pored over these pleas hoping for messages from those they'd lost. No one touched them or tried to remove them. "Ella hoped to find one from us or my parents, but there was nothing there," said Jowita. Nor could she find out what happened to their brave caretaker Mr Wróbel, or to Ms Nitecka or Miss Paulinka from their apartment, but all are convinced that if the two old women survived the war Ms Nitecka would have remained loyally with her mistress until the end.

At the site of Pawiak Prison, there were more desperate notes. German bomb squads had demolished the building in August 1944, less than a month after Ella was freed and Zula deported. All that remained was a fragment of the entrance gate bearing the Pawiak inscription, and a single elm tree – the last living testament to all those who suffered behind the prison walls. On a pile of rubble, wedged between chunks of bricks and mortar, stood a makeshift cross. Almost all of the prisoners had been sent to the camps or murdered by the time the building was deliberately blown up, and most of the doctors released. On the morning of July 30, the Nazis tied the hands behind the backs of 1,800 male and female prisoners and forced them to run through the ghetto ruins to the railway sidings where cattle cars waited to take them to Ravensbrück and Gross-Rosen camps. Packed tight into the wagons, people cried out for lack of air and water but the Germans simply opened fire on the wagons, killing many of those inside. Some 90 kilometres from Warsaw, the train stopped and the dead and dying were transferred to one wagon, which was set alight, burning some alive. Their charred bodies were buried in a mass grave beside the track.

The remaining 107 inmates of Pawiak were executed by firing squad two weeks later within the ghetto ruins, including two women with babies born during the Uprising. The Germans only spared the last remaining doctor, a nurse and the kitchen staff, but one week later two of the kitchen staff were murdered anyway, including a woman who was seven months pregnant. The news filtering back to Warsaw from Nazi concentration camps including Ravensbrück and Stutthof was equally as shocking, and far worse than Ella could have imagined, with the calculated genocide of millions of men, women and children, killed in the cruellest of ways.

The only building still standing in Warsaw that had any meaning for her was her adoptive grandparents' apartment in Saska Kępa, but homeless immigrants had since taken it over and refused to let her in. With no shelter, food, or water in the city, she didn't know what to do at first but eventually found lodgings at 10 Inzynierska Street, where someone named Rahower vouched for her – perhaps a relative or a surviving member of the Home Army. After waiting fruitlessly for news from Zula or anyone, after several months she finally left Warsaw with a heavy heart and drifted north to Łódź, the city of Zula's birth, where she'd heard that Jewish survivors were congregating. The town had been virtually undamaged by the war and had become the temporary headquarters of the Polish government, as well as a billet for some of the liberating troops. Ella remained there for a few more months, trying to decide what to do and where to go next.

Jowita said, "In the spring of 1945 immediately after the war Ella looked for us in our old apartment, which did not exist anymore because that entire part of Warsaw lay in ruins. Having been unable to find any of us, she went to Łódź where Jewish survivors gathered." From there Ella learned that there were special Displaced Persons Camps being set up in old Germany army barracks and former concentration camps across Europe for the homeless and orphans like her. With no money, only the clothes she stood up in and no other choices open to her, she decided to go to one of them.

Ella's choice was a DP camp in Landsberg am Lech in Bavaria, where some of the new friends she had made in Łódź had already moved to. The camp had been liberated by the US army in April 1945, and once turned into a DP camp became one of the most influential in the network for Zionists hoping to emigrate to Israel. Some 7,000 survivors had gathered there to digest the bitter fact that they had no homes to return to and that there was no one waiting for them. Now that the war was over the shock and the sense of loss was overwhelming. The DP camps gave them a place to take it all in before finding the strength to embark on a new life. Ella arrived alone in Landsberg in June 1946.

In Lower Silesia, where Pamaja, Jowita and Kalina had been little more than unpaid slaves overseen by cruel and unfriendly Germans for the previous ten months, the news that the war was over came one day after the event. A unit of the Polish Army arrived in their village and triumphantly told them the news. It was May 9, and they said, "The peace treaty was signed yesterday. Today, we march on Berlin!"

Pamaja immediately packed up their scant belongings and set out on foot with the children to look for their parents in Warsaw. "She told us, 'We're going home. We're going to find your mama and your papa.' I was so happy. I couldn't wait to see them." The journey took over two weeks and when they arrived in the devastated city they could hardly believe their eyes. "After five years of war, we didn't think anything could shock us anymore but this was a terrible shock. The city was a catastrophe. Our house no longer existed. It was in ruins, with only one floor standing. Those beautiful old streets were blackened and charred."

Like Ella, they could find no evidence of any member of their family alive and were met only by the thousands of fluttering notes pinned to the ruins. Pamaja wrote one to Artur and Zula to let them know she and the children were alive, and she stuck it to what was left of their building. Then the sorry little trio made their way to the temporary wooden bridge the Russians had made to span the river. Heading for Saska Kępa, an area that had remained largely unscathed, they hoped to find the children's grandparents alive, but were further shattered to discover squatters in their once lovely home. "There were lots of strangers there and they wouldn't let us in," Jowita said. "That, too, was so shocking. I asked my mother about them years later and she said to me, 'My dear, there are always people who will fight to the death and then there are the others who will steal everything they can.'"

Pamaja, who was not well and had already done so much to keep the children safe, somehow found the reserves to take them on to her cousin on the other side of the river. This woman kindly took them in for three days until they were stronger. As soon as Pamaja heard that some of the city's railway tracks had been restored and there were a few trains running again, she managed to find one to take them the 130 kilometres to Mława. Once there, she prayed that she would find her sister and brother-in-law, the kindly shoemaker Mr Bieńkowski, alive.

Mława, too, was barely recognisable to them after so much shelling and fighting. The Germans had blown up the main square and Artur's KKO bank. Moshe Złotnik's grain store was nothing but a hollow shell. The town's synagogue and Jewish schools had been burned on the first Yom Kippur after the German invasion, and the streets were still littered with the debris of war. The parish priest Władysław Maron, whom Artur had nicknamed 'Little Tomato', had been killed in 1944, and the spirit of the town seemed crushed. Someone was living in their parents' apartment and refused them entry. Fortunately, Pamaja's sister welcomed them with open arms and immediately started to take care of them in her family's little wooden house at number 8, Stary Rynek, on the corner of Niborskiej Street and the main square.

"It was a typical artisan's home," said Jowita. "It looked like a little chapel and felt like something from the 17th century. The walls were covered in crosses and holy pictures and photographs of two Popes. The old man led prayers every evening. He had his workshop in the kitchen and there were two rooms, one big, one small. He and his wife moved into one small room and gave us the larger one to share. Mrs Bieńkowski told Pamaja, 'Mr Artur and Mrs Zula did so much for our family and especially for Stanislav. We don't have much, but food and shelter we can give the children. They can stay as long as they need to.'" And they did.

In Malmö, Sweden, Zula was given the refugee number 8544 and, with almost 600 other women, was sent straight into quarantine for two weeks at schools in the medieval coastal town of Landskrona, some 40 kilometres away.

She was frail and thin, still recovering from her illness and from the physical and mental ordeal of waiting for death in a prison and concentration camp for over a year. She was desperate to get back to her children but had no choice but to spend the next ten months in Sweden. Like many survivors of the war, she was unable to leave because she didn't have a passport or any documents that identified her, and the verification process in a chaotic Europe took months.

Determined to do something useful once she emerged from quarantine, she signed up to work in a factory making light clothing. She had travelled from Ravensbrück with a 21-year-old Polish girl called Irena Możdżeń, whom she had befriended early on in the camp. Irena was a first-year medical student in the city of Łódź when she was arrested in 1940 for being a member of the Home Army. She had been in prison or camps ever since and, after five years at the hands of the Nazis, she had almost forgotten how to behave beyond their walls. Just as Zula had cared for Ella, so she cared for Irena and the pair became inseparable. They decided to learn Swedish 'so as not to go mad' while they were waiting for their travel papers to be approved, and Zula had insisted that the orphaned Irena should return home with her, where she would continue to take care of her.

Paweł and Jadwiga Kaliniecki finally emerged from their cold, damp Warsaw cellar after eight months in hiding, whereupon Jadwiga, aged 64 and suffering from rheumatism, found that she could hardly walk. Within days she fell over and broke her hip badly. In a ruined country whose hospitals had been destroyed and whose largely Jewish doctors had all been murdered or sent away, she received inadequate medical attention and was left crippled for life.

"She never walked again," Jowita recalled. "My grandfather, who was 70, had to leave her when he went to reclaim his home, but the squatters refused to let him into what they and the Russians had turned into a squalid, vermin-infested hole. They threatened him and he was too weak to fight them so he had to flee. They were homeless and my grandmother was disabled and they still had no idea if their daughter and grandchildren were alive. It was a terrible time for them both."

Ella, still fearing that all of her beloved Pieńkiewicz family had perished, eventually found sanctuary in the DP camp in Landsberg, 65 kilometres west of Munich. The second largest camp of its kind in a former German army garrison in what was by then the American Zone, it was designed for some of the 250,000 people like her who found themselves without anywhere to live. The purpose of the camp was to provide food, shelter and a community that would support her as she recovered from the trauma of war and began to think about rebuilding her broken life. To begin with, Landsberg was a camp for anyone who had been displaced, but from October 1945 it was designated for Jews only and at its peak, it held more than 5,000 people.

Landsberg also became a field headquarters of the Organisation for Reconstruction and Training, which offered education from primary school to college for those children whose schooling had been interrupted by war. Ella was quickly encouraged to resume her studies so – with her dream to be a pharmacist rekindled – she was accepted to study natural science at the camp university and completed a first term in 1946. Although she struggled to learn English, she also found work for the United Nations Relief and Rehabilitation Administration (UNRRA) and then the Munich office in charge of arranging illegal passage to British Mandate Palestine, which had reduced the numbers of immigrants allowed in after the war, fearing a flood.

Once again, Ella was alone in the world, with no one and nothing to her name. All she possessed were the clothes she stood up in. Her only hope at that point was that her family in Palestine might take her in. After all, that was where her mother always intended her to be sent after she'd finished her studies. She also prayed that Zula's parents might have survived and wondered if they could care for her. Desperate to find them and anyone else who might have survived, she registered their names with the International Committee of the Red Cross and the Search Bureau organised by the Control Commission for Germany. Then she started to write heartfelt letters to her mother's sisters Lonia and Dvora and her Uncle Nathan in Palestine, and to Zula's parents in Saska Kępa in the hope that they might somehow receive them even though they were no longer living at their address. In one, she explained:

My aim right now is to reach Palestine. My aunts wrote that they were doing everything to prepare a brighter, better future for me and that only there would I start a new free life. I work here in a UNRRA office and I'm learning English. It's very hard to work without knowing the English language.

One of the happiest days of Ella's life came in early 1947 when she received a letter back from her 'grandparents' that they, the children and Zula had all survived the war, and that Zula had recently returned to them from Sweden. Ella responded immediately:

Auntie, Grandparents, when I am writing to you right now I feel clearly how my heart constricts so much that I am breathless. It is an unexplainable feeling that combines itself in pain, emptiness, and yearning. Oh my God, how much do I want to be able to see you and hug you, Auntie Zula.

Did you know that in the hardest time of my life when I was standing on the edge of the precipice, when I was missing those who were the dearest, in my heart you are the closest person in the world to me? I never had a chance or maybe the courage to tell you that during the hardest time of my life you are my everything to me – my mother, my protector, my friend. I remember the moment of my release from Pawiak... the separation. If you only knew of the terrible emptiness and sorrow I felt when I was leaving the prison walls because I was leaving you within them. Later on when I was free like the others and walking down the street freely I felt a heavy weight upon me – a weight that was crushing me and was not giving me peace. I felt as a criminal who escapes to freedom by paying for it with another's life, a life that was more worthy than hers.

Then the news that you are alive, that you left with the transport of prisoners has brought me back my calm. I don't know if you will believe me. I'm not trying to embellish my words; I am writing as simply as I am thinking right now. I only regret that because of my limited vocabulary I'm unable to describe fully my feelings for you and yours. It was unfortunate that I was unable to see you before my departure from Poland. I only recently learned about your return. Never mind. The world is not coming to an end yet, there are years to be lived and I believe that we will meet again.

Zula's letters back to the young woman she saved have been lost, but Ella responded to them with emotion and affection. In one, written in October 1947, she wrote:

My dearest Auntie, I have finally received the long-awaited and desired letter from you. While reading it I understood that you, Auntie – just you and no one else – are the closest and the dearest person in the world to me. I did not realise it myself until recently but your letter cleared everything to me. Do not misunderstand me. But such a long separation and then my own daily troubles have superficially erased the memories. However, it took only one letter from you to refresh them again. I saw it all again – your experiences, mine, and ours. And through all this I hear your words from the letter – 'Save Elizabeth. She is after all innocent'. One does not ever forget words like that. Since I received your letter yesterday, I have not stopped thinking of you personally and of all of you. I'm remembering all of you and the time I spent with you. When thinking of you I have this weird feeling in my soul and it seems as if I have left a part of my soul with you. All my friends here know you all very well from my stories. Sometimes when I feel like reminiscing I simply bore them to death with my stories of you. Anyway, it is really very simple as everything I have lived through, everything I remember, now is strongly connected with you. The time I lived with you has left an unerasable mark on me.

Right now, I am quite seriously thinking of travelling further. When that will happen I do not know yet. I know one thing, although I do not want to believe it, that I do not know if we will ever see each other again. I have tears in my eyes just thinking about it. I would really like to see you all again, to hug you, kiss you. I wonder if you feel the same. I feel it all much stronger because I am all alone. How is my dear grandma? How is Grandpa? Is everyone in good health? What is going on with the kids and Miss Maria. As I write I see you all in my mind. I feel as if I were talking with you, laughing with you. Forgive me for this letter being so incoherently written. It is because I am in a hurry as my go-between is in a hurry to leave. You will hear the rest. Kisses for all. Ella.

Later, she wrote again:

I have been walking with this letter in my hand a smile on my face and I've been telling my friends that I finally received a letter from my auntie. The whole yesterday evening I was telling my friends gathered at my place about you. Know that for a few hours you were the focal point of attention and I have finally had a chance to express everything that was bursting from me since I got your letter. Yes Auntie! Maybe it was ill advised that I left without seeing you. But right now I have impression that it is too late to come back. I have taken a step (I don't know if it is forwards), I have set a goal and it would be too difficult to turn away from my chosen path. I have been constantly receiving letters from my family in Palestine who want to see me there and have made considerable effort to realise that goal. Last week I received a visa to France obtained via my parents' old friends who have been living there for quite a while now. If I'm not mistaken they were pressured into doing it by my family in Palestine, who insist that I move to France. Supposedly it is easier to leave for Palestine from there. I have not fully decided yet but, if I do decide, I could leave within a week, not longer.

She went on to tell her about her work in the office of the International Refugee Organisation, and how she was still struggling with languages. She spoke of a 'wonderful vacation' in the mountains of Berchtesgaden near the Austrian border and enclosed a photograph of her there. In return, she begged for one of Zula. She ended her letter: *Kisses for you, grandparents, kids and Pamaja. I think of you always.*

As time passed, the Russians, who took over control of Poland, made communication with its citizens more and more difficult. The new leadership became obsessed with spying and contact with a Western country was treated as an act of espionage. As a consequence, many of the further letters between Zula and Ella went astray or were destroyed unless they were in praise of the new regime. Ella recalled later: "Right after the war Zula was writing and begging me to come back to a better Poland. She had always been a socialist and she became a party member." Then the letters fizzled out, but Ella kept writing:

I've sent letters several times by different ways, but I do not know if you have received them. It is awfully difficult to make contact with Poland from here. Just because I have not written to you for such a long time does not mean that I have forgotten about you. I'd have to not be human to forget about you, whom I owe so much, whom I owe my own life.

Zula walked back into her children's lives in time for Christmas in 1945. For the previous few months, they had been adjusting to being back in Mława, albeit in a very different kind of existence from the one they'd known before. Pamaja had continued to take care of them and to further their interrupted education, and it was she who maintained contact with Paweł and Jadwiga, and eventually with Zula too, once she was discovered to be in Sweden.

"We completely lost touch with Mummy during the war and didn't know for a long time if she was alive or dead. The same went for my father. Then we heard that she was alive but far away, so there was a long time that we didn't see her – and didn't know if we ever would," said Jowita. She remembers their eventual reunion as a happy one, although she was sad and disappointed that Artur wasn't with her. "Mummy said Daddy would be home soon, and that we should keep praying that he was safe and well. When I asked Pamaja, 'And what of our cousin Ella?' Pamaja said, 'Ella? She is not your cousin. She was a girl your parents took from the ghetto and they had no place to put her so she had to live with us, even though it was against the rules of the Home Army.' I was so surprised as I'd believed everything my parents told me."

Zula also went to visit her parents, Paweł and Jadwiga, whom she hadn't seen since her arrest in 1944. They were shocked by each other's gaunt and haggard appearance. The Kalinieckis were still unable to return to their own home because of the squatters in their apartment, an injustice Zula was not prepared to accept. Jowita said, "Mama wasn't very big but she was such a strong woman and she went to their apartment and she mobilised all my grandparents' neighbours and they forced the people to leave. It was relatively easy and much harder to get rid of the vermin they left behind. The place was in a disgusting state, infested with bedbugs and fleas, so she had to clean it up before her parents could return, but they did – and my grandmother took to her bed."

In time and because of the new political boundaries that had been drawn up across Europe, all contact between Ella and Zula, East and West, was lost. Exhausted and grief-stricken, each of them had to spend what little energy they had left on planning a new future for themselves. For Ella, at least, there was some good news in that she now had someone to share that future with. Ephraim Perkiel, known as Romek, was almost exactly the same age as she was, born in Poland two weeks earlier on May 1, 1924.

The pair had known each other from afar in the Warsaw ghetto, where Romek had resided with his father Chanina, a jeweller, his mother Chana and two brothers Zvi and Lulek on Nowolipie Street, just a few streets away from the Złotnik family rooms. In the ghetto Romek had been a volunteer for the joint Jewish Distribution Committee, the secretary of the Jewish Youth Committee, and he also worked as an underground teacher. In his late teens, he smuggled food and messages in and out of the ghetto and in February 1943 he escaped and lived in Warsaw with false papers to work with the Polish underground. Just before the Ghetto Uprising in 1943 the SS arrested his father and brother Lulek beyond the ghetto walls. Romek, fearing that they wouldn't survive in the camps without him, gave himself up to be with them. Both were murdered in Treblinka, along with his mother, who had been transported there earlier.

Between the years 1943-45, Romek somehow managed to survive eight concentration camps in Poland, Germany and Czechoslovakia before ultimately being liberated by the Americans from Mauthausen in Austria. He was listed in many of the Nazi documents charting his journey as a metal worker by the name of 'Israel Perkel'. This is because the name Israel was given to many Jewish men by the Germans and the name Sarah to women, and the Germans often misspelled the surnames.

After the war, Romek had travelled to Landsberg in search of the only surviving member of his immediate family, his young brother Hersch, known as Zvi, born a year after he was. Romek found Zvi – who was soon to leave for Palestine – and then he found work as a translator with the American authorities, who were searching for Nazi war criminals. A keen tennis player, Romek was reacquainted with Ella when she accompanied a girlfriend to a tennis match he was playing in. Always the joker, Romek told the young women, "I love tennis. While everybody else was looking for food in the camps after liberation, I was looking for a racket!"

As someone who spoke six languages – English, Polish, Hebrew, Yiddish, German and some French – Romek soon became head of the immigration department at the Jewish Agency for Palestine in Landsberg, working in the same building as Ella. The pair fell in love and were married in Munich on May 27, 1948 – the Jewish date *of Lag b'Omer*. Ella wrote later that all their friends attended, and everybody was happy. "We were dancing and singing and being normal... It was wonderful." Her plans to emigrate to Palestine and join her relatives in Tel Aviv in what was about to become the State of Israel wavered on meeting

Romek, who was considering emigrating to the United States instead.

Ella's Zionist resolve faltered still further when the Israeli War of Independence began on May 15, 1948, following the creation of the State of Israel. They were shelved altogether on June 9 of that year when she heard the tragic news that her 44-year-old Aunt Dvora – who had been writing to Ella and begging her to come – was killed when her Tel Aviv home was bombed by an Egyptian plane. Although Celina Złotnik's sister Lonia was still urging the couple to come, and Ella had fond memories of her elegant Aunt Lonia from Mława, it seemed too risky a move to make. After six years of conflict in Poland and so much suffering, the newlyweds still hoped to get to Israel eventually but on the week that they hoped to leave the trains in Europe went on strike, and their plans changed. With Ella newly pregnant, they decided to go to America instead. Their son Mitchel said, "When my father wanted to get something done, he generally did. He'd accomplish it by hook or by crook. Once they knew Mom was pregnant with me, he declared that his child would not be a German. He wanted it to be an American citizen instead."

It wasn't easy to get into the United States after the war and anyone who applied needed to prove that they had a sponsor who would house them and find them work. Ella had a relative Eddie Landau who vouched for her in New York. Romek's best friend from the camps, a man named Joseph 'Joe' Tekulsky, was already in New York so his aunt and uncle Philip and Pauline Mashenka sponsored Romek. This, and Romek's record of assistance to the US authorities in Landsberg, confirmed by the CIA, secured their visa.

Pregnant and suffering from morning sickness, on April 17, 1949, Ella and Romek boarded the USAT *General Hersey,* a former warship that had been repurposed for army transport. It left Bremerhaven in Germany and arrived in New York one week later. Joe Tekulsky and his new wife Isabel were waiting at the harbour to greet them. Refugees, without any money other than that given to them by Jewish organisations, Ella and Romek gave their temporary New York address as 1679, E 3rd Street, Brooklyn, and later moved to a relative's apartment on Fordham Road in the Bronx. The Jewish charities gave all new refugees some money and clothing and they also helped them find work. Romek listed himself on immigration documents as a 'slipper maker'. His first job was sewing slippers and then he found work in a suitcase factory. He also worked for a company that manufactured raincoats, packing them for shipment to customers. By 1952, he and Ella were able to afford the rent on a small apartment in a large redbrick block of flats at 7602, 21st Avenue, in Bensonhurst, Brooklyn, from where they applied for US naturalisation.

Their son Mitchel, named after Ella's father Moshe, was born in a Christian hospital on October 26, 1949. Ella, who was 25 years old, vividly remembered the cross on the wall above her bed. America was bewildering to her at first, as the only English she knew was the little she'd picked up in Landsberg. The rest she learned later from watching American TV, so that she could at least buy food or converse with her children who would grow up American. To her girlfriends she spoke Polish, however, something Romek strongly disliked as he worked very hard to be an American and not identified as a refugee. He dropped the name Ephraim and replaced it with Frank to everyone outside the family and was intent on erasing his Polish accent. The couple only spoke Polish together when they didn't want to be understood. In company, they spoke English.

Romek enrolled at the City College of New York and at the New School for Social Research and became an avid fan of the Brooklyn Dodgers baseball team. He found work at the Herzog Metal Corporation, owned by a relative of Ella's, which he eventually took over when the owner retired. Five years after they arrived at Ellis Island, Ella and Romek Perkiel became American citizens and Romek officially changed his name to Frank (although his family always called him Romek). The date was November 11, 1954, a few months before the birth of their daughter Anita, named after Romek's mother Chana. She was born in Brooklyn on August 25, 1955. The family eventually settled into a community of Jewish Polish survivors in Forest Hills, Queens in New York City.

After Ella's departure to the US and Zula's return to Poland, all hope of contact appeared to be lost. Jowita said, "Mother only found out from our grandparents that Ella went to the US or to Palestine, but she did not leave any forwarding address." Ella continued to write to Paweł and Jadwiga, but by then they had moved out of Saska Kępa to the town of Dzierżoniów in the so-called 'Recovered Territories' in Lower Silesia in support of Zula who'd found work there and moved with Pamaja and the children.

Dzierżoniów (formerly Reichenbach im Eulengebirge) lay at the foot of the Owl Mountains and was renamed after a Polish priest named Jan Dzierżon. Like many towns in the region, it had a chequered history of ownership from Bohemia to the Hussites, from the Austrians to the Prussians and then became part of the German Empire in 1871 until it was transferred to Polish authority after the war. A concentration camp named Gross-Rosen was situated nearby and its 20,000 Jewish survivors, along with other Poles repatriated from the Soviet Union, settled in the new town. Zula and her family were amongst them.

Jowita said, "My mother took us to the Regained Territories in Lower Silesia after the war, because this is where our Warsaw neighbours had taken over a former German engineering factory that specialised in making radio valves. They offered her the job as chief of administrative staff and she had no choice but to accept it, as she had to provide for her parents, the two of us, and loyal Pamaja. She told them, 'But I don't know anything about radios or administration!' and the neighbour told her, 'But you do know about life and you can stop the thieving.' All the Germans had been sent away by decree and new people had been brought in to work at the factory but there was so much theft after the war, because people had become accustomed to it and because the Russians soldiers were determined to go home with anything they could buy or steal. So, all of us went to Dzierżoniów and took two of the German houses that were given to survivors of the camps as gifts for life. Mama's friend Irena had one house and we had the one next door. They adapted them so that they were interconnected. We stayed there for two years."

Irena had come from a wealthy family but after four years in prison and in Ravensbrück, she'd forgotten how to behave. Jowita remembered her watching them to see how they ate food with cutlery and how she would walk around a rug rather than step across it. "She forgot everything she was ever taught before. Mama helped her enormously." With regular employment and enough food, Zula too gradually recovered her strength and sanity and was able to care for her surviving family. Her mother Jadwiga remained bedridden and cared for by a servant, her father Paweł was too old and unwell to work, but helped care for the house and the children, and the girls both enrolled in a local school. "Mama always said she would never start a new library but she did it four times – before the war, during the war, in this place, and then again later. By the time she died she had more than 5,000 books."

Irena, who had no surviving family of her own, became a close part of the family but Zula was concerned for the young woman's future and encouraged her to make a new life for herself. "Irena was 25 and Mama said she should marry so she ended up with a nice man who was a pharmacist. He was ten years older but they had three children and lived in the nearby town and kept in touch all their lives. Irena was one of only five women from Ravensbrück that my mother kept in touch with. She was the eldest and they met every year for a reunion."

In January 1949, less than three years after the war and at the age of 70, Paweł Kalinin Karniewski, later Kaliniecki, a once esteemed bank manager from a noble Russian family, died of a brain haemorrhage caused by heart problems. The nobleman who had lived through the Russian Revolution, reinvented himself, spotted something special in Artur Pieńkiewicz and mentored him to success and then to the altar with his daughter, had no more fight left in him. The telepath who'd adored Zula, frightened his granddaughter Jowita when she was a child, but been a great comfort and surrogate grandfather to Ella in her time of need, was buried in a simple Christian ceremony in remote Lower Silesia.

"Grandfather's funeral was a very modest affair," Jowita recalled, sadly. "Nobody really knew him in that town. Some colleagues from Mummy's factory came and that was it. I have very fond memories of our last summer together when we took long evening walks together in the forest after dinner. I liked to go with him and, as a 13-year-old girl, I asked him all manner of questions about politics and religion and history. He had a simple melody of his own and such pale eyes that were almost silver. I remember he told me that if I ever found that I had powers of telepathy as he had, then I should never use them. He said it would be like throwing a stone into a lake and never knowing what result it might have on another mind or soul. I promised. I realised on those walks just how wise my grandfather was and I always felt very quiet and calm and certain in his company. I now understood why Ella had loved him so. The sad part was that he died before she could find him after the war."

Once Zula had the factory operating to her satisfaction and that of her employers, she focused on her political work within the Communist Party, rising high within the hierarchy and earning herself a nice apartment in the city. But following her public objections to the merging of the Socialist Party and the Worker's Party, she was forced from her job and her home within days and found herself unemployed and homeless. It was a shocking turn of events that left her disillusioned with the socialist ideal that she had been committed to since her days as a law student in Warsaw. "Mother's situation was difficult, because she represented the old socialists from before the war, and honestly believed that socialism should be the right way for Poland, provided it was properly realised," said Jowita.

Along with Irena and her family, in 1948, Zula relocated them all 60 kilometres north to the city of Wrocław (formerly Breslau), the second most ruined city after Warsaw. The place was gradually rebuilt into a fine university town and, although she had no connections there, Zula initially found work as a secretary. Throughout these difficult years, she waited patiently for her husband Artur, always hoping that he might one day return to them from the camps. All she was able to discover initially was that he had disappeared on a death march somewhere after Pölitz.

By January 1945, roughly half of the 50,000 remaining inmates at Stutthof were taken on death marches in severe conditions that killed many of them. The ones that survived were marched into the Baltic Sea. Jowita said, "For 20 years we thought he'd been forcibly drowned in the Baltic from the camp at Neuengamme. Prisoners were pushed out into the water in containers until they sank.

"Some time later, my mother gave an interview to that effect on the radio and a friend of Artur's from Bergen-Belsen contacted her and told her, 'That isn't true. He didn't die that way.' He said that Artur had looked after him during his time in the camps and survived a death march all the way to Bergen-Belsen but then got sick with typhus. When the British came, he ran to my father and told him, 'We are free! We are free!' but all Artur wanted was water to drink. He ran to fetch him some, but there was a lot of confusion and chaos with people celebrating and dancing and he got caught up in it all. By the time he eventually found some water and ran back, my father was dead. He burst into tears and was very tense as he told the story to my sister Kalina and kept saying, 'I could have saved him.' He'd been carrying the guilt for years. She told him not to think that and said that, knowing our father, he would have forgiven his friend."

Red Cross and German records eventually confirmed that Artur had been sent for a time to the heavily bombed shipyards of Stettin (Sztutow), then to a neighbouring labour camp named Hägerwelle at Pölitz, a place where the Nazis sent the Polish intelligentsia, members of the Warsaw Uprising, and any they wanted to discipline for resistance. It also housed hardened criminals. An estimated 9,000 of the 13,000 inmates perished there in brutal conditions with ritualised beatings twice a day – before and after they left the camp to work from dawn until dusk. They were forced into gruelling and dangerous labour such as handling chemicals and unloading coal without gloves or protective clothing, all on a starvation diet of bread and thin soup. The prisoners known as *kapos* who worked for the Nazis in return for extra food and privileges treated them as cruelly as the German guards, and many prisoners threw themselves on the electric fences to escape their ordeals.

According to a Search Bureau record of the Control Commission for Germany filed by Zula's father Paweł in 1946/7, Artur Pieńkiewicz was last seen in Bergen-Belsen, but is believed to have died on April 15, 1945, the day of the camp's liberation by British troops. He was 49 years old.

In 1951, Zula married Feliks Malanowski, a former inmate of Auschwitz and Mauthausen concentration camps, who had ginger hair and freckles and was described as a charming man with a 'sunny disposition'.

Three years older than Zula, Feliks came from a poor family and had grown up in the old town of Warsaw. Married with two children, he and his wife had divorced on his return when they discovered that they had nothing in common. Once Zula had remarried and with the children grown into healthy teenagers, faithful Pamaja decided that she was no longer needed. Much to the family's sorrow, she returned to Mława where she lived with her sister and brother-in-law until her death in the 1960s, although the two families remained in contact and their fondness for and gratitude to Pamaja never waned.

Feliks had been a respected athlete and Olympian before the war, holding the Polish record for the 400- and 800-metre relay races. He'd attended the 1928-Amsterdam summer Olympics where he came fourth and fifth respectively but was then arrested and sent to the camps as part of a systematic plan by the Germans to eliminate the finest sportsmen in Europe and eradicate the competition. He was a kind stepfather to Jowita and Kalina and they often went to him with their problems, rather than to Zula. "I think Mummy needed someone like my father to stabilise her," said Jowita. "She became very moody and we never knew whom we would meet this day: a severe Polish mother, a jolly pal, a sentimental mummy or a wise but demanding teacher."

After the war Feliks became a director of two factories that produced linen materials, and a member of the Workers' Party. An enthusiastic organiser of sporting life in Wrocław, his association with the discredited Zula impacted adversely on his life, however, and the couple found themselves largely ostracised. Then, in the early 1950s, the Polish Prime Minister Józef Cyrankiewicz visited Wrocław to see the rebuilding of the city for himself. He spotted Feliks in the crowd of people in the lobby of an event and instantly recognised him as someone who'd helped him in the camps. Ignoring the dignitaries he was supposed to be meeting, he hurried over to shake his hand and thank him, crying, "Feliks! How good to see you!"

Jowita said, "Apparently, all the senior Party members looked at each other and within two days Mama and Papa Feliks were back in the new Party. Feliks had a new job in a bank as well as his sports work, and Mummy began working in local broadcasting, first as a journalist and then directing the Radio Theatre plays, which she loved and did for 20 years. She was a good director, the radio dramas she directed were usually broadcasted in the Warsaw All-Poland programmes."

In 1953, Jowita's grandmother Jadwiga died, having never walked again since the war. She'd been cared for in her final years by a young Polish girl who adored her and learned much from her about history and life. She told Zula, "I didn't know that there were still such great ladies as this!" Jadwiga was buried in a cemetery in Wrocław where previously only German citizens had been laid to rest.

It was only eight years since the war ended and yet, in that time, Zula had endured so much. She had lost all those closest to her – chiefly Artur and her parents, with Ella and her brother George both in faraway lands. The hopes she'd had for a better life in Poland after the war had been dashed after the Communists seized the family homes, land, businesses and property. She was poor by comparison to her youth and, although she loved her job, she found that working under strict Party rules didn't suit her temperament.

"She was controlled by those high Party members who had been brought in to keep order and observe the rules established by the Regional Committee of the Polish United Workers' Party," said her daughter. "They did not trust or like the more intelligent journalists, especially the ones who freely expressed their views. My mother was once chosen as chief of the local Party but the upper ranks weren't satisfied with her work. With time she became more and more difficult. Her inner sense of justice and need to fight for what was right made her aggressive, both in work and at home. She was much respected, her work was highly appreciated, but she was liked only by those working with her or under her."

All this was a far cry from the woman who'd once turned heads in Warsaw and Montpelier and who had caused ripples amongst the socialites of Mława. Stuck in a place where she didn't feel fully appreciated, frustrated at work, her children growing, Zula must have wondered how her life could have gone so badly awry.

9

REUNION

New York, summer 1963

Ella's life in New York was happy and fulfilled. As well as being a full-time 'Mom', she enjoyed art and sculpture, she loved to travel, go to the theatre and the opera, and became a consummate hostess, a devoted wife and a good friend. But there was always one person on her mind whose absence made her sad eyes sadder – Zula.

None of the letters she sent to Poland were ever replied to, and none of the enquiries she tried to make about any of those she knew and loved, now trapped behind the Iron Curtain, came to anything. She had no idea that Zula and her family were living far from Mława and Warsaw, that her auntie had remarried, or that Artur and both Zula's parents had died. All she had were her memories and the fragile *gryps* that her Auntie had written to her, which she carried everywhere in her handbag.

Then one day in the mid-1950s, at a party in New York, Ella happened to meet a former Polish Air Force officer who, she was told, had fought in the Battle of Britain with the Royal Air Force. "I don't suppose you've ever met anyone called Captain George

Kaliniecki?" she asked innocently, hoping beyond hope for some news of Zula's brother who'd fled to the UK when the Germans invaded Poland in 1939 and joined the RAF.

"Yes, of course!" the British pilot replied with a smile. "I know George very well. Why?"

Ella's heart soared. George would know where Zula was. Although prevented from travelling home for fear of being branded a 'traitor' by the regime, George would hopefully be able to put the two of them in touch. Excitedly scribbling down her home address and new surname on a scrap of paper, she pleaded with the pilot to write to George as soon as possible and pass the information onto Zula so that they could finally reconnect. And so it was that the first letter from Mrs Zofia Malinowska arrived in Queens addressed to Mrs Ella Perkiel. The two women who had meant so much to each other during the darkest days of the war were finally back in touch after so many years of silence.

The news they shared was bittersweet. For the first time, Ella learned of the multiple losses Zula had endured – losses that she, too, felt deeply. Artur had risked so much to take her into their home and had painstakingly coached her about her supposed hometown of Lvov. She remembered happy nights in the Warsaw apartment with all the family gathered around the stove, playing cards, or reading Kipling, as they tried to pretend that the war wasn't pressing in all around them. And her closeness to her Kaliniecki 'grandparents' had given her so much comfort in her darkest days, enabling her to somehow survive the loss of her brother, mother and father.

Ella was pleased to learn that Zula had found someone else to share her life with thanks to Feliks, and happy that Jowita and Kalina were healthy and doing well in school. In her first of many letters back, she proudly told Zula of her happy marriage to Romek, and the births of their two children Mitchel and Anita, and how they had made a new life for themselves in America.

It was clear from Zula's letters back that she still hoped Ella might one day return and resume a life in Poland. She wrote more enthusiastically than she may have felt about life in a communist regime and of her work in the theatre, reminiscing about their days checking coats in the Golden Beehive. Ella never disappointed Zula outright by telling her that she could never imagine returning to Poland to live, but she promised that she would try to visit one day – as soon as this was allowed for someone from the West.

The two women wrote to each other as regularly as they were allowed after that, sharing their stories and tragedies. Telephone contact was impossible at first (there was a 20-year waiting list for a home phone to be installed in Wrocław), even though they'd have loved to have heard the other's voice. Later they were able to speak briefly, but only by going through a censored switchboard and pre-booking the call weeks in advance. Zula's daughters Jowita and Kalina – who had only discovered after the war that Ella was Jewish – also wrote, calling her 'sister'.

The letters between the two families passed back and forth for the next 15 years, despite the frustrations of their messages being intercepted, censored and redacted. Many were lost so the responses were often disjointed or full of recriminations that one or the other hadn't written for too long. When they did reach their intended recipient, Ella was able to tell Zula of her family's first visit to Israel by boat in 1961 when the children were still young. Having sailed there, they were greeted warmly in the port of Haifa by her aunt Lonia and her husband Lulek, who became surrogate grandparents to Anita and Mitchel.

Anita said later, "I remember that visit to Israel so clearly. We went there by boat. There was quite a scene at the harbour as they presented me with a doll and chocolates and were overwhelmed to see my mother, crying and hugging her continuously. To them, she looked like a Hollywood star with her fine clothes, blonde hair and sunglasses. She was treated like a celebrity and she showered them with gifts. From then on, I had the novelty of having an older generation in my life – something I was not accustomed to. They were warm and loving and emotional. Mom told them all about Zula and how she had saved her, so – of course – from that moment on they loved her too."

As the two women continued to send each other photographs,

letters and packages containing gifts, it became clear to Zula that Ella's life was rich and full in America and that she would likely never return to live in Poland.

The summer of 1963 marked a historic period of American history. John F. Kennedy was President, the Civil Rights movement was at its peak, and Martin Luther King Jr delivered his 'I have a dream' speech.

In Forest Hills in the New York borough of Queens, another kind of dream was being realised when Zula Malinowska, formerly Mrs Pieńkiewicz, aged 54, arrived from Warsaw to visit Ella Perkiel, nee Złotnik – the first time the two women had seen each other in almost 20 years. In what was to be an emotional but heartfelt reunion, Ella, by then aged 39, was finally able to introduce her husband Romek and her two young children Anita, eight, and Mitchel, 13, to the woman who'd saved her during the war.

It had taken months of frustrating paperwork and bureaucracy to finally secure the permission needed for Zula to come to America. During an era of heightened emotions about Eastern European Communists, US government officials interviewed Romek on several occasions to ensure that he wasn't secretly facilitating the arrival of a Polish or Russian spy. Anita said, "Someone even turned up at the door to check my father out and ask him many questions to make sure that he wasn't a spy. They really had to jump through hoops to get her to visit and it was frightening for them to be under suspicion for anything after their wartime experiences."

From the moment Zula arrived at their apartment that summer, it was clear to everyone there that the two women had a very close bond. "It was like a mother and daughter relationship – very loving," the children both said. "Zula was a very kind and softly spoken lady who we knew only as the woman who saved our mother's life. She easily connected with people and was charming, sweet and pleasant. Mom loved having her here and being with her. Her visit was one of the highlights of her life."

Despite the language barriers as Zula didn't speak much English, the American-born children called her 'Grandmother' and managed to communicate with expressions and gestures or would ask Ella to translate, which she loved. Anita recalled, "Zula handed me the most beautiful doll I had ever seen, dressed in a multicoloured outfit typical of the girls of Krakow. I treasured this doll and still have her displayed in my bedroom to this day." Zula also gave her a Polish children's book called *Pimpusia Sadełko* about an alley cat. "She read it to me in Polish, sitting with me and pointing out the pictures. I didn't understand the words but somehow I understood the story, and it was nice to have this older lady reading to me like a kind grandmother – something I had never known."

In their two-bed, one-bathroom apartment where Anita and Mitchel shared a bedroom, Zula slept on the couch in the largest room in the flat – the living room. She shared it with a piano that Anita became accomplished at and a television – something she watched avidly throughout her stay, just as Ella had done when she first arrived in New York. "She was fascinated with American TV and loved to watch variety shows and Westerns with us," Mitchel recalled. "We'd all watch together and see her delight."

Ella cooked Zula her signature dishes of meatloaf and roast chicken, and always decorated the table beautifully with matching plates and bowls, flowers and napkins. They went on the ferry to see the Statue of Liberty and for picnics in Central Park with their friends, who had organised themselves into societies in order to socialise, holiday together, play tennis and have fun. There was the Warsaw group and the Łódź group and this huge circle of friends gathered in each other's houses for dances and parties and card games – including bridge.

"They were a great bunch," said Anita. "All of them had come to America with nothing, no families and no occupations but they were hard-working and ambitious high-achievers who were determined to push education for their kids and give them the kind of life they had missed out on." The friends of the Perkiel family welcomed Zula with open arms and accompanied her and Ella's family to Fifth Avenue to watch the Pulaski Day Parade in memory of Polish General Kazimierz Pulaski, who became an honorary American citizen after saving the life of George Washington while fighting against the British in the US Revolutionary War. Zula was astonished that a Pole would be honoured so and had been since 1937.

The children were aware of their parents' history and that their mother's story was unique, but it was never generally discussed. Nor did it feel necessary or appropriate to ask too many questions. The Second World War was a recent and still raw memory for the adults in their lives and the legacy of it surrounded them. The area of Queens where they lived was full of friends Ella and Romek had made who'd all survived similar experiences, some of whom they'd met in the DP camp at Landsberg. They had emigrated to the United States together to become a surrogate family in lieu of relatives. All Mitchel really remembered was 'the lingering fact' that his mother had a brother who'd died, and he had long felt the absence of grandparents when many of his schoolfriends still had theirs.

"We had no blood relations that we were aware of, so we knew that everyone had been lost on both sides, except for my father's brother Zvi. We only knew snippets about the rest and all that I knew came from Dad, who was more forthcoming about his experiences. I remember him briefly explaining that the tattoo he hid under his wristwatch on his right arm (when everyone else wore their watches on the left) came from a time when he was put into a concentration camp. He didn't have the tattoo removed but he didn't like to show it either.

"He did have PTSD and a recurring nightmare in which he was back in the concentration camps – only this time he was fighting to protect us kids. Despite all this, we were a normal American family and then some. My mother was a housewife and my father, who was self-taught, worked very hard and was able to provide for us."

Anita added: "I don't remember ever not knowing about my mother's experiences and about Zula. We were surrounded by survivors so that was my world, my extended family. I spent a lot of time with my mother as a little girl so when she had friends over in the afternoon after school, I'd sit with them in the kitchen and listen to them chatting. My father's story was much harder to digest. I knew horrible things had happened to him and I identified with that, especially if we saw pictures of concentration camps on TV. Mother's story was a beautiful love story, and far more comforting and I gravitated towards that."

By contrast, neither of Ella's children recall her speaking about the war directly to them, chiefly because she wanted to focus on the positives in life. "She was soft and gentle; the kindest most loving person you could ever meet," said her son. "To know her you would never think that she had suffered. She wanted to live in the present, not the past. She was the opposite of my father who was short-tempered and easily angered. He was very protective of us."

One of the legacies of the war for Romek was that he was quick to judge people, perhaps because of his years spent in the camps. If the subject of the war came up, then he would take on an expression that Ella came to recognise and she would quietly whisper, "Let it go." Mitchel remembered one time that his father got angry with someone in their social circle and his mother was trying to calm him down. "He said, 'He's an idiot,' and she said, "Yes, but I love his wife. We were in Landsberg together. Let's just enjoy their company, OK?' She was passionate about being a wife and mother and she loved taking care of us all. She was determined to create a genial environment for us all and was always there, acting as a gentle safety net through any crisis."

Zula took great delight and interest in the cosy home that Ella had created for her little family, which was such a contrast to the imposing Złotnik house in Mława, or to where she'd lived in Warsaw. As a writer and artist herself, Zula was pleased to learn that Ella had developed her creative side and joined several art clubs in which she liked to paint and make things with her hands – which became a kind of therapy for her. Ella's artwork included driftwood shapes, lakeside scenes and, later, alabaster sculptures, although Zula noted that many of the canvases were monochrome and several featured the sad Jewish eyes she'd first spoken to her about after she rescued her from the ghetto.

Every summer for ten weeks the Perkiel family had a custom of taking their vacation in the Dingle Daisy bungalow colony at Monticello, in the Catskill Mountains in upstate New York. They went with a large group of their friends and carried on with their usual socialising. "There was a casino and a multipurpose entertainment centre with games, and all the parents had costume parties and dressed up. There were Shabbat services and movie nights and camp programmes for the kids, including boating on the lake. We could go and have sleepovers or meals at anybody else's bungalow and I have such happy memories of my time there," said Anita.

The colony was on a huge lake where it was far cooler than the heat of the city, plus there was much more for the children to do. Their father would commute the two-hour drive every Friday evening in his white Chevy Impala and drive back on Sunday nights. In 1963, Zula went with them and when the children thought about her visit years later they wondered what she must have made of this wholesome American family, their friends and fellow campers. Perhaps even more interestingly, what did they make of her?

"One thing we got to know right away was that Zula was a staunch communist, which was so alien to us," said Mitchel. It was the peak of the Cold War after the Bay of Pigs face-off between Kennedy and Khrushchev, and Romek told anyone who would listen, "Americans don't understand the Russians; only a Polish Jew does."

Ella had long been stockpiling cans of soup, tuna fish and beans, as well as hiding huge canisters of water under the sink.

"She was stuffing things into any cabinet in preparation for war. Everything was crammed into her tiny kitchen," said Anita. "She was frightened, and that frightened me, although my father never seemed to be scared. He felt he could save us from anything. Even so, he and my mother were glued to the television news and took it very seriously. War had been such a big part of their lives and in many ways it had always been in the background of ours too so, we thought, 'OK, so this is going to happen again, and this is what we have to do.' We were too young to understand what it all really meant, so we kind of took it in our stride."

At school, Anita and Mitchel had to learn the 'duck and cover' drills to prepare for an impending nuclear attack. Mitchel added, "Hiding under our desks with our hands on our heads, we had a very clear bright fear that the Russians were the enemy. Meeting Zula was the first time I had ever heard anyone say that Kennedy was."

While the kids attended summer camp, swam, fished and played tennis in the relaxing setting of the Catskills, Zula and Ella stayed glued to each other's sides, laughing, talking, and enjoying each other's company in the kind of atmosphere that they had never once been able to share in Poland. "I remember it as a time of heightened happiness," said Mitchel. "I never saw them crying or anything like that. They stayed up late, relaxing, smoking and drinking, and sharing the past. There were no tears or high emotions. Everybody was very happy and my mother was thrilled to have her there."

Mitchel said that his mother 'cherished' her relationship with Zula. "They were inextricably tied to each other and to the war, but she found hope in that too. It was in her nature to forgive and move on and not dwell on the horrors. She was the one who would always find the good in people... She never said a bad word about anyone."

Whenever Romek arrived from Manhattan he would often sit on the periphery and listen in to the animated conversations between his wife and their guest. He had all but rejected their native Polish as a language and focused instead of constantly improving his English, which was extremely good and spoken without the accent that Ella was never quite able to shake. He didn't even like her to speak Polish in the house, as it reminded him of a past he preferred to forget, but she had no choice with Zula and the two of them quickly lapsed into a familiar way of speaking.

The more Romek heard about their story, though, the more he realised that it deserved to be told. He decided to do something about it and went to the offices of an American Yiddish-language newspaper called *Forverts* (Forward) where he spoke to the general manager Adolf Held. Held then summoned a Polish-speaking reporter, who wrote later:

When I came into the office, a thin young man was sitting there, 39-year-old Frank (Romek) Perkiel, one of Hitler's victims who had miraculously survived Hell. He told me 'I will not speak today about my own bitter experience at the hands of the Nazis. ...I want to tell you my wife's story. It is a most remarkable story of a daughter of Israel who survived by posing as a Christian girl. She also survived infamous Pawiak Prison in Warsaw where she was imprisoned with her Christian rescuer, an exceptional Polish woman... Now this woman has come to New York from Poland. We brought her here for a visit. She is like a mother to my wife and my wife is like her own child. She is one of those Christians who put their own lives at risk in order to rescue Jews from the hands of the German murderers.'

Romek started to tell their story but then he stopped, telling the reporter, "It will be much better for you to hear the whole story from them – my wife and this exemplary Polish woman. Come to my house. Here is my address." The reporter did as requested in late September when the family returned from vacation and he started to take notes: "The late summer evening was cool in the pleasant neighbourhood. At the door I was greeted by two women, one young, with a pretty face but eyes filled with pain. The other, a typical Aryan Pole with deeply set creases on her face."

Romek told him, 'These are the two heroines of the story.'

He said, "Pictures painted by Mrs Perkiel hung on the walls of the elegant house – portraits with sorrowful eyes. The house was well appointed, tidy and bright, but suddenly the mood changed. As the women started telling their story an air of distress overtook us and as the young Mrs Perkiel – the first to speak –began, dark shadows crept over the walls."

The two women then recounted the whole story, explaining how Zula and Artur worked for the underground, and how they first decided to save Ella from the ghetto. "The love and warmth that was around me in that home made me feel like a member of the family," Ella said, before Zula added, "She was like our own child. I decided then that if she was sent to her death, I would go with her."

The reporter said that the women sat together and talked deep into the night, reliving the dark years of the war. He noted that Zula had brought Ella a large book of photographs published by the Polish government entitled *Battle, Death and Memorial.* "Both look at the agonising images and told each other, 'We could easily have been part of that mountain of ash and bones.'"

Before the reporter left, he was introduced to Mitchel and Anita, who listened to some of what the women had spoken about with sorrow in their eyes. In the final sentence of his report, he wrote:

The boy points to Mrs Malinowska and says to his little sister, 'This woman, our new grandmother, is an angel. She saved our mother's life...'

Zula returned to Poland a new woman. She came back with boxes of American goods and seemed happy and uplifted by the whole experience, according to her family.

She could see how adored Ella was by Romek and her children and how successful she had been in creating a happy, loving home life for her growing family in spite of her own tragedies. The couple were giving their children a happy normal American childhood and filling their lives with art, theatre, travel and music. Romek was, by his own admission she said, 'an encyclopaedia of humour' and a gifted speechmaker whom people would always ask to make the toast. He made up limericks with his children and was blessed with great comic timing and delivery. Ella was quieter and far more observant, but she still possessed that enviable poise and inner tranquillity she'd had since childhood.

Jowita said, "Mother came back delighted. She told me that she always treated saving Ella as the most important thing she did in her entire life, but now she knew that she not only saved someone's life – she saved a wise and good woman, appreciated and loved by many people.

"She saw how respected and loved she was, with the accent on the first. This was an unusual position for someone with no profession or great wealth." Her view was expressed by Zula herself in the interview she gave to *Yiddish* newspaper, in which she said: "Whatever I did in my life there was one thing important that I did. I saved Ella – and now that I have been to see her in America, I know that I saved not only a good dear girl but a wonderful woman."

Jowita, then aged 31, said that she and the family were very poor at that time and Ella had been so generous with her gifts to them all. "She brought back so many things for my son Igor, who was just one year old – things that he could wear right up to the years five or six. There were three beautiful pairs of short trousers and all kinds of other quality clothes that would be good for three summers. Then she sent baby equipment and all kinds of things that she thought might be helpful."

Zula told her that Ella had 'a lovely home, a lovely family, lovely children and lovely friends,' all of whom thanked her for saving Ella. "She had travelled to France and Germany for her work so I don't think there was much that shocked or surprised her about America, but she was impressed by the kind Jewish community and by the effort they all made to make her feel so welcome."

When Jowita read the article written in the Yiddish newspaper about Ella and Zula, she was shocked. "The journalist wrote that Ella was saved because of the love my parents felt for her, which was so intense that it made them risk our entire family's life to save her. When in truth it was just common decency – human compassion. My father didn't ponder long whether he should do it or not. He barely knew Ella, but he knew he had to go and help them. They were simply being responsible human beings who could not leave a child to a certain death. The love for Ella came later, once she was with us."

After Zula had returned to Poland, Ella asked Romek to accompany her to a New York notary's office so that she could make a sworn declaration of just how much Zula had done to help her and others during the war. This may well have been at Zula's request, as such a letter would help with her standing in the Communist Party. The typewritten single-sided document signed and dated October 11, 1963, set out the story of how both Zula and Artur rescued not only Ella and Moshe from the ghetto, but tried to save her brother too.

"During my whole stay in the house she surrounded me with selfless care," she swore. "She treated me as a daughter even though hiding Jews was punishable with a death sentence not only to her but to her whole family and two little daughters... I state that it is only due to the effort and care of Zula Pieńkiewicz that I am alive, and that during my whole time spent at her house was I offered a witness to her humane and generous disposition to those Jews persecuted by the Nazis, despite the danger. This testimony I meant to present to the government of the People's Republic of Poland because of the creation of a new medal for saving Jews in the years of 1939-45, which medal – to the best of my knowledge and conviction – citizen Zofia Pieńkiewicz-Malanowska deserves fully."

———

Over the coming years, contact between the two families escalated and Kalina, who wrote to Ella often and sometimes telephoned, travelled to New York a few years after Zula with her husband Zjbicek to meet Ella's family and friends.

Ella's daughter Anita recalled, "Kalina was very pretty, like a doll. I was about 11 years old when they came to visit, and she was very kind to me. She and her husband were actors who specialised in plays in the language of Esperanto and they performed one in my parents' home. They created a little theatre and asked my parents to invite their friends for whom they put on a one-act play. Everyone donated something towards their performance so they were able to make a little money from it."

Kalina loved reconnecting with the big 'sister' she remembered from the war and was so impressed by how stylish and beautiful Ella had become, dressing herself in matching items of clothing that looked as if they were couture even though they weren't. Even her friends sought Ella's opinion when it came to clothes, as she seemed to know just the right thing to wear and when. This was a throwback to her Mława childhood when she and her brother Ishay had all their clothes handmade by a local dressmaker and their shoes made – no doubt – by the talented Mr Bieńkowski. Their mother Celina, who was equally stylish, was determined to keep up appearances in the town.

It was in 1970, on her business trip to London with Romek, that Ella had her emotional reunion with Jowita in their hotel, sobbing over the poem that about Ella's escape from the ghetto that she still carried after being given it by Zula the day she left Pawiak. When the two women eventually parted, their tears dried, the two of them promised to stay in touch.

As the threat of a Cold War lifted and the chances of travelling to Poland increased, Ella decided to go back for a visit at last. She and Romek had moved into an apartment in Manhattan by then and were enjoying winter holidays in the Caribbean and Venezuela with survivor friends, visiting family in Israel, ski trips to upstate New York and Canada, and world cruises. She went on spa breaks to Florida and to visit her girlfriend Ala Biberkraut in Munich and other dear friends in Europe and the south of France each summer. One year she applied for a Polish visa and travelled to Warsaw after Nice. It was her first time back in the country in 30 years.

Many of her friends were surprised by her decision. Like Romek, they had turned their backs on Poland. It was his reluctance to go that prevented Ella from going sooner or more often. He was not alone in feeling that it would be too traumatic to go back to a country where they had lost their families and all that they possessed. Despite her initial misgivings about returning, the trip went well and Ella was made to feel most welcome. She avoided Mława and the places in Warsaw that would have been too painful to revisit and focused instead on spending 'family' time with Zula and Feliks in Wrocław, as well as Kalina, Zjbicek and Jowita, meeting Zula's only grandchild Igor, about whom she had already heard so much.

Now that the two young girls whose lives had been so intertwined during wartime were grown women, there was more time for Jowita and Ella to reflect back on some of the events that had befallen them. They were difficult memories for them both. "Jowita had also suffered a lot," explained Ella's daughter Anita. "She remembered with great fondness the father that she had lost and she was much more painfully aware than Kalina that their mother was taken away from them for so long, also feared lost. She had seen things during the war that affected her deeply and she had gone through so much and sacrificed a lot. Like my mother, her childhood had been lost the day the Nazis invaded and – by the time the war was over – she was already an adult, even though she was still physically a child."

Jowita is more philosophical and said, "The war sits deeply in our lives but we do not live with it constantly. We all made a life after the war, and it was all right. Sometimes it bursts out, but it usually sits deep inside." Each time she saw Ella, it was natural that the war should feature prominently in their conversations, as she was able to fill in some of the gaps that Jowita didn't know or hadn't wanted to ask her mother, who sometimes spoke of her time in the Resistance but rarely spoke of the war.

During their many discussions, she told Ella in all honesty, "Everyone so admired your fortitude and calmness and your courage," to which Ella expressed immediate surprise. "Fortitude? Courage? But I walked all over Warsaw so tense from fear that it still stays with me today."

Later, she told Jowita that when she left Poland after that first trip, she was on the plane to Paris when she heard an announcement by the captain welcoming passengers to French airspace and immediately felt a huge flood of relief. "Suddenly my entire body relaxed, releasing the tension that had lasted for the two weeks I was in Poland, even though I didn't realise it."

The legacy of the war still ran deep in them both.

EPILOGUE

Zula was diagnosed with terminal lung cancer in 1976 at the age of 67. She treated the news with typical stoicism, but her husband Feliks fell apart. He was completely devoted to his vibrant, courageous wife and, like many survivors who had married fellow survivors, he had leaned on her heavily for emotional support after the war.

Unable to imagine life without her, Feliks killed himself in April 1976. He was 75. Once again, Zula had lost a husband and the children had lost a father in a tragic way. With the hourglass turned and Feliks buried, Zula did something unexpected and decided to throw a party for her surviving girlfriends from the camps.

She had never lost touch with the seven women who were her best companions in Ravensbrück, including Irena, and when she discovered that she would die of cancer within a few months, she threw a party and invited them all. Jowita prepared everything for them at home and took Igor out for the day and came back late in the evening, expecting it to be over. To her surprise, she found them all having the time of their lives. "It was the most hilarious women's party I had ever seen – quite an event, and one that nobody could ever repeat. They celebrated from breakfast to dinner and were playing and singing and happy together. When I told them, 'But I thought you'd be sad!' they cried, 'Why should be sad? We are all still alive!'"

Zula's health declined quite quickly after that and Jowita had to manage caring for her at home, along with her own work in Polish theatre, and looking after her 12-year-old son. Kalina and her husband lived and worked in a town 30 minutes away but when Jowita called and said she could no longer cope, they came immediately and were 'wonderful'. As Zula's pain increased and she became dependent on morphine, she began to call out for Ella. Her affection for the Jewish girl she'd protected ran so deep that she wanted her at her bedside even as she was dying.

Ella, forever grateful to the woman who'd saved her life, knew that she had to say goodbye to Zula and flew in from New York to be at her bedside. Zula was semi-conscious when she arrived, but she opened her eyes and said, "Are they here, all three? Are all three here?" Jowita assured her that Ella was there with her and Kalina, and Zula slumped back on her pillow with a smile. "She was happy. She knew Ella was there," Jowita said. "She had asked for her to come."

Ella sat with her two 'sisters' Jowita and Kalina until Zula eventually lost consciousness, and then – with a heavy heart – she flew home. Zula died a few days later, on February 8, 1977. She was 68 years old. Ella said afterwards, "We were family. It seemed like she wanted to see me before she died. When I arrived, she could hardly talk anymore, but she'd waited and then she died."

Four years later, the Yad Vashem World Holocaust Remembrance Center in Jerusalem recognised Zula and Artur Pieńkiewicz as 'The Righteous Among The Nations'. Ella's daughter Anita, who'd requested the honour, wept when she received the letter that said:

We are happy to inform you that at its meeting on December 2, 1981, the Commission for the Designation of the Righteous decided to confer on the above the highest expression of honour, a medal and the right to plant a tree in the Avenue of the Righteous on the Mount of Remembrance in Jerusalem.

The Śliwczyński family was also recognised.

In 1983 Anita and her husband Mark Sarna, whose parents also survived the Holocaust, travelled to Jerusalem together. There, in the Garden of the Righteous Among the Nations Gentiles, they planted a pine tree for the couple who had saved Ella's life. Then in 1987, two years before the fall of Communism in Poland, Ella and Romek invited Jowita to stay with them at their apartment at 200 East 57th Street in New York. It was 17 years after their chance reunion in London and Jowita was able to secure a travel permit to the United States thanks to the more relaxed atmosphere pervading Eastern Europe at that time. The thing that struck Jowita the most about Ella's home was how lovely it was and how many plants she had that seemed to bring the garden inside. "All my life plants were only to be grown outside but Ella had one corner that was beautiful, like a garden. I will never forget it."

Jowita saw Ella for the first time in her new home and finally appreciated her many qualities; qualities that had been constantly held up to her and Kalina by Pamaja when they were children. "From amongst the strong people I know she belonged to a very small number of those who did not feel the need to impose their strength, opinions, or plans for life onto others. She was a vivid observer, but I did not hear her start a discussion about her or someone else's opinions, especially controversial – she most likely preferred to avoid reefs of disagreements and shoals of common beliefs; she left her interlocutor with his opinions without questioning them and kept her own to herself."

In the relaxed surroundings of the Perkiel apartment in a non-communist state, the two women spoke again of their memories of the war, many of which were still extremely painful. Jowita revealed for the first time how Mrs Złotnik had telephoned Zula and made her promise to protect Ella a few hours before she allegedly committed suicide, something Ella had never previously been told.

"I thought my mother should have told Ella about this, but she didn't want to," said Jowita. "I do not know why. In my opinion, the choice of such death would be Mrs Celina's act of pride and courage worthy of remembrance in the family. In the end, Mama agreed that I should relay this to Ella during my stay in New York. Ella took this information with mistrust: just like me she couldn't understand why my mother had never told her this herself. Maybe she was unsure of her supposition, since all she had to support her idea was only that telephone call from Mrs Celina."

Jowita said that so many years had passed from those events that they sometimes spoke about them 'as of a book read a long time ago.' She added, "On the surface we talked indifferently, until suddenly there came up some still very important but not yet tamed episode, like that farewell between Ella and her mother, which caused her pain until the end. We both had to be careful then; such matters still lived somewhere deep down in each of us."

Ella told Jowita, "We only tried at that time to survive." Although she and Romek had become less religious since the war and Ella believed there was too much hatred and emotion tied up with religion, they respected the faith of their late parents and instilled the traditions of Judaism into their children's lives. They celebrated the Jewish holidays and took them to visit their families in Israel and remained proud Zionists.

Romek embraced Judaism more fully later in life but in the 1980s he was focused on living his life and making a living and enjoying his survival. Just a few years earlier, he had drawn up a document which he'd headed 'Biographical Material', perhaps with a view to publishing his perspective on Ella and Zula's story. After listing his personal details and life and work experiences, he chronicled some more personal matters: *Recreational activities: humorous poetry, travel and tennis. Enjoying: close friends, brother, daughter-in-law, grandson, good company, absorbing theatre, competitive (but not brutal) sports, fascinating speakers, **most of all**; my wife, my daughter, and my son. Being turned off by: liars, phonies, those who use many words to say very little, wicked people, flagrant injustice under this or any other name. Maxim: to attain my share of the material and spiritual goods this world has to offer. I do not crave any more than my share, but I shall not settle for any less.*

In New York Jowita had several interesting conversations with Romek about faith that she found refreshing. "Finally, someone talked to me about Judaism without emotion," she said. "Ella believed that life has to be lived and given its whole sense here on earth without relating to life after death, even if it exists. From the further course of our conversation, it transpired that after her experiences during the war she referred to matters of faith rather indifferently, just like many people from her generation.

"Romek, who during that conversation had just came home and was mixing us drinks, was a person who knew religion well since childhood. He told me that for him religion matters to the extent that it binds the Jewish community, its tradition, culture, and sustains its continuance." One of his opinions that shocked Jowita was his declaration that, although he was thankful to Zula and Artur for saving his wife and admired their readiness to help people, he himself could not risk the lives of his entire family for strangers and would not have let Ella do so.

"In his opinion our father also had no such right. He claimed that a man, as head of a family, answers to God and society for the safety and prosperity of his family, which is given to him as a saintly duty. He explained to me that according to the rules we have obligations firstly towards God and religion, secondly towards the family, and lastly towards our community. This appeared very foreign to me because, according to the rules we were taught, we have obligations towards God, honour and our country, including sacrificing our own lives. Romek believed that this could bring an entire society to extinction as we learn from the example of Warsaw Uprising, when the entire city lay in ruins and more than 200,000 people died. According to Judaism the life of even one person is already the life of the entire nation and is worth keeping at any price. At this point Ella had enough and started making dinner, hence we ended our philosophising."

Anita, then aged 32, visited Jowita at her parents' apartment and took three-year-old Danielle and baby Ilana to see her. Jowita was delighted to meet Ella's grandchildren, the two new members of the next generation whose lives would be forever linked. It quickly became apparent to Jowita then that Ella had hardly ever discussed the details of the war with her children. Although they lived with the legacy of it in Ella's over-protectiveness, they didn't fully understand the events.

Anita said, "My mother did suffer from separation anxiety when it came to me especially. I was the only one of my friends who had a curfew – they still laugh about it – and had to call my mother all the time to let her know where I was and with whom. There was no normal baseline for me. I felt like I couldn't ever complain that I was 'starving' or 'freezing', and when one of my kids came home with head lice my mom was very upset. 'We had lice in the ghetto,' she exclaimed. 'But that was because of all the dirt and the filth. I didn't expect this in America!'"

When Jowita returned to Poland she wrote to Anita and began to recount her memories of her visit. She spoke of a moment when she was reminiscing about wartime events, and someone asked why the Germans would shoot at Polish children. *"I felt then as a person who, speaking with someone in his room, opens the door to the balcony and suddenly sees that there is no balcony, but 20 storeys of an abyss and a strange, unknown street."* She said that she began to question how someone brought up in America might imagine life in Warsaw during the war and became convinced that some believed it to be relatively normal where people led a quiet life, unless they angered the Germans, and the hell was only in the ghetto. *"Ella – your mother – was silent. After you had left I asked her why she hadn't told her children anything about the war."*

Jowita decided that one day she would sit down at her computer and chronicle the events as she remembered them, to fill in the gaps in their knowledge of all that had happened in Poland between 1939-45 and before. Her son Igor had asked her to write down everything anyway, so now she would have an extra reason to do so. In a later letter to Anita, she added, *"In the history of our families we have a beautiful theme, which we develop and which maybe our children will continue to develop.*" But first there was one last visit by Ella, Romek, Anita, Mitchel and his wife to Poland to see Kalina and Jowita. It was in the late 90s when Ella's health had already started to decline.

"It was the last trip my mother took with us," Anita said. "Not long afterwards, Kalina died young of cancer too, so we were glad that we got to spend time with her." Mitchel, who had never visited Poland before, was eager to go with his wife. "We visited Auschwitz and Majdanek, which was very sobering as my father showed us where he'd been held. We went to Młava and Warsaw, which I remember as being relatively pleasant as opposed to being sombre. Mom showed us where her house would have been – it wasn't there anymore. Then in Warsaw she took us to where she had lived with Zula and we visited the site of Pawiak and went through some of the archives and found her registered under the false name."

Anita said that later that night they all had dinner in the hotel and Ella suddenly announced that she wanted to go to her room – claiming she had 'a strange feeling'. Anita followed to check on her. "I think that was a catalyst moment for her. Going back was hard. She looked at me and said, 'I am never coming back here again.'"

Years later, as dementia and Parkinson's disease started to affect her cognitive function, Ella became fixated on the loss of her pocketbook in which she had always kept Zula's poem and a few of the little *gryps* written on flimsy cigarette papers in Pawiak. The bag went missing on a house move to Florida and after that Anita says her mother never quite recovered emotionally. "She was devastated by that and never quite the same. It was the last link and the start of her decline. The light went out, the curtains closed, and she became silent and unresponsive. She couldn't talk for the last two years of her life; there were only tears."

Just as with Feliks when Ella became ill her husband broke. Romek's life raft was sinking, and he didn't know how to go on without her. Suffering from depression he would survive his wife by only a few years after a series of strokes.

Ella Perkiel died on August 22, 2000. She was 76 years old. She was buried in Mount Hebron Cemetery in Flushing, Queens. Her gravestone, in English and Hebrew, reads: 'Ella Perkiel. *Yocheved, daughter of Moshe Złotnik and Tsipora Frenkiel.* Born in Mława, Poland. Survivor of the Shoah. Beloved Wife, Mother, Grandmother and Friend. You Lit Up Our Lives'.

To the end of her days, she remained grateful to Artur and Zula Pieńkiewicz for giving her the gift of life and the many happy years that she would never otherwise have had. She survived the war to marry, see the world, watch her children grow up and to enjoy her six grandchildren. Her son Mitchel said that the greatest gift she gave them all was love. "My mother's legacy was one of forgiveness and not looking back. It was what helped her remain so serene all her life." Anita added, "I learned so much from my mom. She was soft-spoken yet had a strong and determined personality. She understood right from wrong, while being very forgiving. She was an admirer of all art forms and was a creative and talented artist herself. She was a wonderful friend to everyone in her life, including me. I am blessed to call her my mother."

Of her relationship with Zula, Anita said, "Theirs was a remarkable and beautiful bond, borne out of war. Zula and Artur paid such a high price for their resistance work and for hiding my mother. We are all of us grateful for their courage, self-sacrifice and devotion. Our bond with Zula's surviving family is lifelong. We consider them our Polish family."

In 2008 Anita went to Jerusalem with Jowita and her family to show them the burgeoning tree planted there in her parents' honour and memory. It was during that visit that Jowita told them that if the tables had been turned, she knew that Ella would have done all she could to have saved them from the Nazis. She shared one especially poignant memory of being with her in Poland on one of her first visits there after the war. "We stood in front of a mirror side by side doing our hair before leaving the house," Jowita said. "Looking at the two of us in the reflection, and me with my Slavic features, I said, 'Which one of us looks more like a Jew? Ella smiled and said, 'You, of course, but don't worry. If someone wanted to kill you, I would hide you.' And I knew in my heart that she would have."

Years later, long after Ella had died, her grandchildren Danielle, Ilana and Ari visited the relevant sites in Mława and Warsaw with Jowita. Afterwards Ilana asked Jowita quietly, "Tell me, during the six years of the war did you ever smile once?" Thinking about her innocent question and of all the things that happened to both families after the Germans crossed the border into Poland on September 1, 1939, Jowita and Anita, the two descendants of the Złotnik and Pieńkiewicz family, looked at each other knowingly. Instinctively they both felt that it was finally time to tell the full story of the girl with the sad eyes and the courageous woman who had given Ella her heart...

ACKNOWLEDGMENTS

I am indebted to Anita Perkiel and her husband Mark Sarna for inviting me to research and write the unique and precious story of Anita's mother Ella Złotnik and her family. From the moment we met in Washington, DC in July 2017 – thanks to our mutual friend, the inimitable Nadia Ficara at the United States Holocaust Memorial Museum – we made an immediate connection.

I knew straight away that it would be a tremendous privilege to chronicle Ella's story and that of her courageous saviours Zula and Artur Pieńkiewicz, but I also knew that it would be a difficult story to research because of the wartime need for secrecy. Anita, who accompanied me for much of my research in Poland, proved to be the perfect travelling companion and co-researcher, as we delved deep into the past together. Her husband Mark has also been nothing but supportive and encouraging, and her brother Mitchel Perkiel was generous with his memories of his parents and of Zula's momentous visit to the US in the 60s.

Zula's daughter Jowita and her son Igor Pietraszewski in Wrocław made my task infinitely easier with their unfailing patience, generosity of spirit and warm welcome. Jowita not only allowed me access to her own written account of the war but for hours at a time over many days she graciously shared her memories of Ella and her own parents and their experiences. In Warsaw and Mława, she flew in to accompany us to all the places that had an important link to her family's remarkable story. As she told me, "I did well in my life not to go back to those times. It was something black and bad and dark. There were so many clouds and it brings it all back. I didn't want to go back to this time until years later when my son Igor asked me to write it down for him and his children. And, of course, for Anita and hers." At times, the burden of legacy was almost too much and it was difficult for Jowita to talk about some of the saddest events, but she was determined to keep going and always allowed me to gently press her for more.

Also in Poland, I am indebted to Andrzej Puchacz for his translation, fixing and chauffeuring roles, and especially for his passion for this story. I must also thank my friend and occasional translator Anna Slotorsz for her unfailing support and assistance. And Jarosław Janiszewski for his excellent research on our behalf, providing photographs and archive material from Mława that I would never otherwise have found. Similarly, my thanks to Magdalena Grzywacz and Krzysztof Napierski at the Mława town archives, to Klara Jackl at the Polin Museum of the History of Polish Jews in Warsaw, and to the helpful archivists at the Oneg Shabbat Archive and the Jewish Historical Institute. Polish author Sebastian Pawlina was generous with his time and information, and in Warsaw Malgorzata Kozikowska kindly helped me with information about her grandparents the Śliwczyńskis.

Blanka Wilchfort and Ilana Lewitan kindly shared some information about the Biberkraut family in the Warsaw ghetto with the Złotniks, and Tomasz Lesniak of the Department of Collections at the University Library in Lund, Sweden was helpful with my research about the survivors of Ravensbrück. Archivist Silvia Rathmann helped me at Bergen-Belsen, and Dr Sabine Arend at Ravensbrück.

Special thanks to Jo-Ellyn Decker, Research and Reference Librarian at the United States Holocaust Memorial Museum for her endless patience with my numerous requests for documentary proof. And to Dvora Meneshof, a cousin and friend of Anita's, who kindly shared with me her own research into their family and especially their background in Mława, Poland, which proved to be helpful and informative. Professor Leonore Weitzman from the George Mason University took time out of her busy schedule to share her memories with me of meeting Ella in 1994 when researching her book *Women in the Holocaust* and gave me permission to use the transcripts.

PHOTOS

Ella as a baby in Mlawa

Ella as a child

Ella with her parents Celina and Moshe Złotnik

Ella and her brother Ishay

Ella, second from the left in school

The Frenkiel family store in Mlawa

The Zlotnik home and store Mlawa

Zula prewar

Respected banker Artur Pieńkiewic

Zula and Artur's apartment block in Mlawa

Zula the hostess

The faithful servant Pamaja

*Zula and Artur with his beloved daughters Jowita and Kalina
before the war*

Zula with Kalina

Zula with her two daughters

The remains of Artur's bank after the German invasion 1939

The remains of the Zlotnik house after the invasion

Zula in the theatre during the war

A prison cell at the feared Gestapo HQ in Warsaw

The feared Pawiak prison, Warsaw

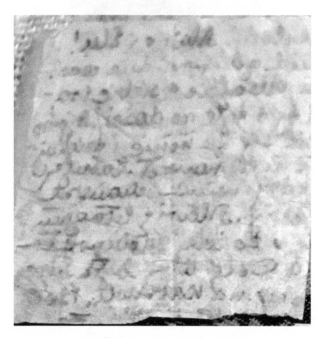

One of Zula's gryps or notes from prison

Pawiak's memorial tree that survived so much

The building where Moshe Zlotnik hid and was betrayed

Ella at the DP camp after the war

Romek in his concentration camp uniform post-war

Ella and Romek as a young couple

Zula after the war

Ella and Romek in 1967

Ella and Zula reunited

Ella with Zula and Kalina

Ella reunited with Jowita

Ella with Zula in New York

Zula in New York with Anita

Kalina, Ella, and Zula in Poland

Ella and Romek at a black tie event

Romek and Ella on holiday

Ella's grave in Queen's, New York

Ella and Romek standing at the tree planted in honor of Zula and Artur, Yad Vashem, Israel 1990

Zula and Anita, Ella's daughter, in the Warsaw park where Zula saved Ella from the ghetto

BIBLIOGRAPHY AND OTHER SOURCES

All Hell Let Loose, The World at War 1939-45, Max Hastings, Harper Press, 2011

Defying Hitler, Sebastian Haffner, Orion, 2002

Forgotten Voices of the Holocaust, Lyn Smith, Ebury, 2005

If This is A Woman, Sarah Helm, Little, Brown, 2012

Holocaust, The Nazi persecution and murder of the Jews, Peter Longerich, Oxford University Press, 2010

Never Again, A History of the Holocaust, Martin Gilbert, Universe Publishing, 2000

No Greater Ally: The Untold Story of Poland's Forces in WWII, Kenneth Koskodan, Osprey Publishing, 2009

Pawiak: Martyrdom and Heroism – Regina Domańska, Warszawa, 1978

Poland betrayed: The Nazi-Soviet Invasion of 1939, David Williamson, Pen & Sword Military, 2009

Ravensbrück: Berattelser Stories, Kristian Lindström, Beretninger, 2017

Rising 44: The Battle for Warsaw, Norman Davies, Macmillan, 2003

Secret City: The Hidden Jews of Warsaw, 1940-45, Gunnar Paulson, Yale University Press, 2003

Survivors of the Holocaust in Poland: A Portrait Based on Jewish Community Records 1944-1947, Lucjan Dobroszycki, Routledge, 1994

The Eagle Unbowed: Poland and Poles in the Second World War, Halik Kochanski, Harvard University Press, 2012

The Hidden Children: Secret Survivors of the Holocaust, Jane Marks, Piatkus, 1994

The Holocaust Sites of Europe, Martin Winstone, B Tauris & Co Ltd, 2010

The Holocaust: A History of the Jews of Europe During the Second World War, Martin Gilbert, Henry Holt & Co, 1986

The Righteous, Martin Gilbert, Corgi, 2003

Trails of Remembrance: 50 Years of The Museum of the Pawiak Prison. Ślady Pamięci, Museum of Independence, Warsaw, 2015

When Light Pierced the Darkness: Christian Rescue of Jews in Nazi-Occupied Poland, Nechama Tec, Oxford University Press, 1986

Who Will Write Our History? Samuel D. Kassow, Penguin, 2009

WEBSITES

- *United States Holocaust Memorial Museum* (http://www.ushmm.org)
- *Yad Vashem* (http://www.yadvashem.org)
- *Jewish Virtual Library* (https://www.jewishvirtuallibrary.org/)
- *Janusz Korczak International Society https://www.korczak.org.uk/associations.html*)
- *The Museum of Jewish Heritage* (www.jewishgen.org)
- *Information Portal to European Sites of Remembrance* (www.memorialmuseums.com)
- *Holocaust Educational Trust* (www.het.org.uk)
- *The National Holocaust Centre and Museum* (https://www.holocaust.org.uk/)
- *The Educational Website Holocaust CZ* (http://www2.holocaust.cz/en/main)
- *The Imperial War Museum* (www.iwm.org.uk)
- Shoah Foundation video testimonies (https://sfi.usc.edu/full-length-testimonies)

ABOUT THE AUTHOR

Wendy Holden was a respected journalist and war correspondent for eighteen years covering news stories around the world, including the Middle East, the USA, and Eastern Europe. She is the author of three novels and more than thirty non-fiction titles, most of which feature inspirational people and many of them international bestsellers. They include *Born Survivors*, the story of three mothers who hid their pregnancies from the Nazis; *Tomorrow to Be Brave* about the only woman in the French Foreign Legion, soon to be a film; *One Hundred Miracles* about a musical prodigy who survived three concentration camps, and *Behind Enemy Lines* featuring a French Jewish spy, now an award-winning documentary.

Wendy's first novel *The Sense of Paper* was published by Random

House, New York. Her second, *The Cruelty of Beauty*, is published in Europe and is to be made into a TV film. She also wrote *Mr Scraps*, a novella about the first search and rescue dog in the London Blitz. She lives on a small farm in Suffolk, England, with her husband and two dogs.

www.wendyholden.com

Dear Reader,

If you have enjoyed reading *I Give You My Heart,*
please do leave a review on Amazon or Goodreads.
A few kind words would be enough.
This would be greatly appreciated.

Alternatively, if you have read my book as Kindle eBook
you could leave a rating.
That is just one simple click,
indicating how many stars of five
you think this book deserves.
This will only cost you a split second.
Thank you very much in advance!

Wendy

FURTHER READING

The series **Holocaust Survivor Memoirs World War II** by Amsterdam Publishers consists of the following autobiographies of survivors:

Outcry. Holocaust Memoirs, by Manny Steinberg

Hank Brodt Holocaust Memoirs. A Candle and a Promise, by Deborah Donnelly

The Dead Years. Holocaust Memoirs, by Joseph Schupack

Rescued from the Ashes. The Diary of Leokadia Schmidt, Survivor of the Warsaw Ghetto, by Leokadia Schmidt

My Lvov. Holocaust Memoir of a twelve-year-old Girl, by Janina Hescheles

Remembering Ravensbrück. From Holocaust to Healing, by Natalie Hess

Wolf. A Story of Hate, by Zeev Scheinwald with Ella Scheinwald

Save my Children. An Astonishing Tale of Survival and its Unlikely Hero, by Leon Kleiner with Edwin Stepp

Holocaust Memoirs of a Bergen-Belsen Survivor & Classmate of Anne Frank, by Nanette Blitz Konig

Defiant German - Defiant Jew. A Holocaust Memoir from inside the Third Reich, by Walter Leopold with Les Leopold

In a Land of Forest and Darkness. The Holocaust Story of two Jewish Partisans, by Sara Lustigman Omelinski

Holocaust Memories. Annihilation and Survival in Slovakia, by Paul Davidovits

From Auschwitz with Love. The Inspiring Memoir of Two Sisters' Survival, Devotion and Triumph Told by Manci Grunberger Beran & Ruth Grunberger Mermelstein, by Daniel Seymour

Remetz. Resistance Fighter and Survivor of the Warsaw Ghetto, by Jan Yohay Remetz

The series **Holocaust Survivor True Stories WWII** by Amsterdam Publishers consists of the following biographies:

Among the Reeds. The true story of how a family survived the Holocaust, by Tammy Bottner

A Holocaust Memoir of Love & Resilience. Mama's Survival from Lithuania to America, by Ettie Zilber

Living among the Dead. My Grandmother's Holocaust Survival Story of Love and Strength, by Adena Bernstein Astrowsky

Heart Songs. A Holocaust Memoir, by Barbara Gilford

Shoes of the Shoah. The Tomorrow of Yesterday, by Dorothy Pierce

Hidden in Berlin. A Holocaust Memoir, by Evelyn Joseph Grossman

Separated Together. The Incredible True WWII Story of Soulmates Stranded an Ocean Apart, by Kenneth P. Price, Ph.D.

The Man Across the River. The incredible story of one man's will to survive the Holocaust, by Zvi Wiesenfeld

If Anyone Calls, Tell Them I Died. A Memoir, by Emanuel (Manu) Rosen

The House on Thrömerstrasse. A Story of Rebirth and Renewal in the Wake of the Holocaust, by Ron Vincent

Dancing with my Father. His hidden past. Her quest for truth. How Nazi Vienna shaped a family's identity, by Jo Sorochinsky

The Story Keeper. Weaving the Threads of Time and Memory - A Memoir, by Fred Feldman

Krisia's Silence. The Girl who was not on Schindler's List, by Ronny Hein

Defying Death on the Danube. A Holocaust Survival Story, by Debbie J. Callahan with Henry Stern

A Doorway to Heroism. A decorated German-Jewish Soldier who became an American Hero, by Rabbi W. Jack Romberg

The Shoemaker's Son. The Life of a Holocaust Resister, by Laura Beth Bakst

The Redhead of Auschwitz. A True Story, by Nechama Birnbaum

Land of Many Bridges. My Father's Story, by Bela Ruth Samuel Tenenholtz

Creating Beauty from the Abyss. The Amazing Story of Sam Herciger, Auschwitz Survivor and Artist, by Lesley Ann Richardson

On Sunny Days We Sang. A Holocaust Story of Survival and Resilience, by Jeannette Grunhaus de Gelman

Painful Joy. A Holocaust Family Memoir, by Max J. Friedman

I Give You My Heart. A True Story of Courage and Survival, by Wendy Holden

Flower of Vlora. Growing up Jewish in Communist Albania, by Anna Kohen

Zaidy's War, by Martin Bodek

In the Time of Madmen, by Mark A. Prelas

The series **Jewish Children in the Holocaust** by Amsterdam Publishers consists of the following autobiographies of Jewish children hidden during WWII in the Netherlands:

Searching for Home. The Impact of WWII on a Hidden Child, by Joseph Gosler

See You Tonight and Promise to be a Good Boy! War memories, by Salo Muller

Sounds from Silence. Reflections of a Child Holocaust Survivor, Psychiatrist and Teacher, by Robert Krell

Sabine's Odyssey. A Hidden Child and her Dutch Rescuers, by Agnes Schipper

***

The series **New Jewish Fiction** by Amsterdam Publishers consists of the following novels, written by Jewish authors. All novels are set in the time during or after the Holocaust.

Escaping the Whale. The Holocaust is over. But is it ever over for the next generation? by Ruth Rotkowitz

When the Music Stopped. Willy Rosen's Holocaust, by Casey Hayes

Hands of Gold. One Man's Quest to Find the Silver Lining in Misfortune, by Roni Robbins

The Corset Maker. A Novel, by Annette Libeskind Berkovits

There was a garden in Nuremberg. A Novel, by Navina Michal Clemerson

Aftermath: Coming-of-Age on Three Continents, by Annette Libeskind Berkovits

The Girl Who Counted Numbers, by Roslyn Bernstein

The Butterfly and the Axe, by Omer Bartov

The series **Holocaust Books for Young Adults** by Amsterdam Publishers consists of the following novels, based on true stories:

A Life in Shelter, by Suzette Sheft

The Boy behind the Door. How Salomon Kool Escaped the Nazis, by David Tabatsky

The Precious Few. An Inspirational Saga of Courage based on True Stories, by David Twain with Art Twain